I CAN BARELY TAKE CARE OF MYSELF

Tales from a Happy Life Without Kids

JEN KIRKMAN

Simon & Schuster

New York London Toronto Sydney New Delhi

Simon & Schuster
1230 Avenue of the Americas
New York, NY 10020

First Simon & Schuster hardcover edition April 2013

SIMON & SCHUSTER and colophon are registered
trademarks of Simon & Schuster, Inc.

For information about special discounts for bulk purchases,
please contact Simon & Schuster Special Sales at 1-866-506-1949
or business@simonandschuster.com.

The Simon & Schuster Speakers Bureau can bring authors
to your live event. For more information or to book an event
contact the Simon & Schuster Speakers Bureau at 1-866-248-3049
or visit our website at www.simonspeakers.com.

Designed by Esther Paradelo

Manufactured in the United States of America

10   9   8   7   6   5   4   3   2   1

Library of Congress Cataloging-in-Publication Data
  Kirkman, Jen
    I can barely take care of myself : tales from a happy life without kids /
  Jen Kirkman.—1st Simon & Schuster hardcover ed.
    p.   cm.
    1. Kirkman, Jen, 1974– 2. Comedians—United States—Biography.
  3. Television comedy writers—United States—Biography. 4. Childlessness—
  Humor. 5. Adulthood—Humor. I. Title.
    PN2287.K672A3 2013
    792.702'8092—dc23
    [B]   2012033097

ISBN 978-1-4516-6700-4
ISBN 978-1-4516-6701-1 (ebook)

THIS BOOK IS DEDICATED TO MY PARENTS.

I love you both and thank you for never getting in the way of my dreams. To my dad, for always saying that women are funny and anyone who doesn't agree can go pound sand. To my mom, who reminded me, "Just think, if we didn't decide to have kids, you wouldn't be here living a fun life and writing this book." Thank you both for having me. Ew, I don't want to think about how I was made.

P.S. Also, thank you for being so overprotective that I never got pregnant as a teenager.

THIS BOOK IS *NOT* DEDICATED TO . . .

one of my schoolteachers. When I told you I wanted to be a writer someday, you patted my head and told me to sit down. When I wrote an original short story about a zombie who wore "Calvin Klein jeans," you told me to write something more serious and that writing funny things isn't good writing. When I wrote a poem and chose to read it in front of the class and then got made fun of for it—you took me aside and said, "When other people don't like what we're doing—it's best to not keep getting up and doing it."* You were wrong.

*True story.

CONTENTS

INTRODUCTION

I'm sitting on my couch in just a bra and sweatpants. For some reason I also have a cocktail ring on my right finger and a feather headband atop my head. I'm too embarrassed to wear the feather-band outside of the house—although I guess not too embarrassed to commit to print that I'm wearing it *and* knee-high pom-pom slippers late at night. When I'm on a writing procrastination binge I start playing dress-up, and I just got bored and quit halfway through, so now I'm procrastinating my game of dress-up by finishing writing the introduction to this book. This is just one example of what it is to be me. Besides the usual distractions from life—friends calling in tears because they're heartbroken, flat tires, deaths in the family, leaks in the ceiling, work—I pretty much have the ability to do whatever I want, whenever I want because I don't have children. That's not the only reason why I don't want children—it's just one perk.

And yes, I don't *want* children. As far as I know, I *can* have children. But I'm not great with kids and the thought of raising them scares me—it's more terrifying to me than an empty house in the woods or a clown doll sitting in a chair. You're just so screwed if you find yourself in any of these situations! There's no way out!

Most people assume that "doing whatever I want" includes partying all night and enjoying my hangover without a toddler sitting on my head. But I'm actually pretty mild. I got nervous one time after taking Benadryl three nights in a row to fall asleep. I fantasized about whether I would have to call my loved ones *before* checking in to Betty Ford or would someone from the rehab center go through my iPhone for me?

I remember asking my mom when I was little if I could go live at this place in Boston called "The Home for Little Wanderers." I didn't realize that it was a facility for orphans. It sounded to me more like a place for free spirits who knew that even if they loved where they were one moment, that could change tomorrow. One thing I know about myself is that everywhere I go is my new favorite place. And I'm not a cold, heartless vagabond either. If in my wandering I end up reading to children at a zoo in Madagascar—wonderful! I don't hate kids. I just hate the idea of dragging a kid around with me as he or she is forced to adapt to my lifestyle. I also don't want to have to carry animal crackers around in my purse.

I have a picture of my cat from childhood, Mittens, on my living room wall. He's been dead for twenty-four years. When friends ask me why I don't just get another tuxedo cat, I say, "I loved Mittens because my mother changed his cat litter. Not me." I do have a small collection of stuffed-animal tuxedo cats given to me as gifts by people who, I assume, assumed that I needed *something* to care for. But those kitties are smashed down facefirst in a wicker basket in the bedroom. I'm afraid to look. I think they might be dead.

The way most people feel about loving being a parent is exactly how I feel about *not* being a parent. I love it. And I can't imagine my life any other way. I'm one of those people in an ever-growing movement called childfree by choice. I think it's a clinical and defensive name for what sounds like an otherwise fun group of people. I've never actually seen members of this movement all in one place. I guess we're not as organized or fabulous or as into riding floats as gay people. We live in pockets of cities and suburbs all across America and the world and we may not have anything else in common with one another except that none of us right now has a toddler saying,

"Mommy, please put a shirt on. It's inappropriate to sit around the house in a bra and why is there a peacock on your head?"

So while I sit here on my couch at home dressed like someone halfway to senility, I'm remembering the time that I was sitting on a couch in my psychologist's office, wondering whether it was weird that I still had my sunglasses on my head during our session. I wondered whether I was too accessorized for sitting around figuring out my problems and analyzing my patterns. It feels like I should treat therapy like going through airport security (which I do a few times a month as a traveling stand-up comedian)—I should have nothing in my pockets, no shoes and no jewelry around my neck, nothing on my outside that can distract the person in front of me from seeing what I look like on the inside.

That day I said to my shrink, "I feel like an outsider in the world because I never want to have children. When people ask me if I want children and I say no—they always say things like 'You'll change your mind.' I'm sick of it and I feel like I don't fit in." I don't know what I expected my therapist to say—probably her usual: "Was there a time in childhood when you felt like an outsider? Is this pushing any old buttons? You know if it's hysterical, it's historical." What I didn't expect was that she'd say, "You don't want kids? Why not? What's up with that?" *What's up with that?*

"Oh no," I said. "Not you too! You're going to tell me I'm weird for not wanting children?" She explained that it's my reaction to those people that we need to work on—and that we don't need to attach any jumper cables to my biological clock. She suggested that instead of answering, "I don't want kids," that I should simply say, "It's not in my plans right now." Oh boy. She had no idea what I was up against at every cocktail hour/wedding/shower/holiday party I've been to since I started to ovulate. I'm convinced that people who want kids and people who have kids have secret meetings where they come up with their talking points. There's not one response to "I'm not having kids" that I haven't heard and I've heard the same questions and comments approximately one bazillion times:

- If you don't have kids, who is going to take care of you when you're old? *(Servants?)*
- Men have to spread their seed. It's in their DNA. *(He can spread his seed all he wants. I have a magic pill that prevents it from growing.)*
- But it's the most natural thing you can do as a woman. *(So is getting my period every month.)*
- That's selfish. You can't be immature forever. *(And spending your days watching* Dora the Explorer *with a kid is mature?)*
- You have to replace yourself on earth. What will you leave behind? *(There are a few plastic bags that I never recycled . . .)*

Random people who want me to have children are the same type of people who won't let up on me because I haven't watched *The Wire* and I never plan to. I just never got into *The Wire*. Is *The Wire* brilliant and life altering and does it make you feel less alone at night? Yes! That doesn't mean I have to like the show. I have no opinion on *The Wire*. It is just not a part of my life. I'm not trying to be cool or different. A Non–*Wire* Lover is not my identity. I just don't even think about *The Wire*. And yet people continue, "It's available on Netflix!" "I understand that it's easy to get." "You'll love it." "I won't. I might. I don't care." "How can you not watch it? Well, what kind of shows *do* you watch?" What will happen to these people if I never see *The Wire*? Are they at home feeling a phantom pain in their abdomens and thinking, *If Jen would only watch* The Wire, *this bad feeling would go away*. And in the same way my Netflix queue remains *Wire*-free, people seem really agitated that my womb remains baby-free.

I took my therapist's advice and started getting cagey with my answer. But once I started saying, "It's not in my plans right now," it was taken as, "Yes, I plan to have kids someday." And then just to avoid arguments, I went through a phase of lying. "Yes. I want to have kids someday. I want to have kids right now. Anybody have a turkey baster? Let's kick this party up a notch. I'm ovulating!" But I'm not going to lie anymore.

I've always been a little different. I was called a "freak" in high school because I wanted to be on a stage instead of on a lacrosse field. I went to a job interview at an office straight out of college wearing black tights, green nail polish, and clear jelly shoes. I got the job but my new boss took me aside to explain the office dress code. She asked me, "What were you trying to prove with that outfit? Why do you want to look weird?" I had honestly thought that this was a good outfit to wear. I wouldn't even know how to try to be weird. It seems like too much effort. Just like trying to be normal—whatever that looks like—often seems more trouble than it's worth. I mean, who really wants to wash her car in the driveway every Sunday (or even have a driveway)?

My favorite TV show when I was six was *The Lawrence Welk Show.* I wanted to grow up and live in a world of bubbles and polka music someday. I went to the most popular girl in school's slumber party in the sixth grade dressed as Groucho Marx. (It didn't go well— you'll read all about it.)

It may not be filled with bubbles and polka (actually thank God for that, my aesthetic and musical tastes have changed), but I've found a community of weirdos in the comedy world. I moved by myself to New York City and Los Angeles. All of my family and my childhood friends live on the East Coast. I decided to wander the country in search of a career as a stand-up comedian. Fifteen years later and two comedy albums in, I'm doing just that for a living, in addition to writing and appearing on *Chelsea Lately* and playing the part of myself in the *Chelsea Lately* spin-off *After Lately.* My days consist of writing comedy and the occasional phone call to my sister to explain that the e-mail she just received from me saying "I'm pregnant, please call Mom" was really from Chelsea Handler, after she'd had her way with my computer.

My twelfth-grade teacher Mr. Bergen would be proud of me. He wrote me a card when I graduated from high school that said in big black letters, **GET OUT OF THIS TOWN. GET OUT WHILE YOU CAN,** and a lovely note on the inside that encouraged me to follow my dreams because he could tell that I wouldn't be happy trying to conform on any level. Now, I don't think having a child makes you a conformist and I don't think that not having a child makes you a nonconformist—but I do think that following your heart no matter what other people have to say takes a real sense of self. My friend Shannon, who has two children, says that the judgment never ends. She had children—she did the supposed "normal" thing—and still people chastise her for not having six kids or for the fact that she doesn't abide by the latest parenting trends. "What? You breast-feed before sunrise? Oh no. You'll end up with a *vampire.*"

The bottom line is that the choices we make often make sense to us but can confuse others. Somebody is always going to be disappointed with your life choice, and my rule of thumb is that as long as *I'm* not the one who is disappointed, I can live with that. If you've ever been thought of as selfish and immature or told "you'll change your mind" about anything, I hope this book can be your card from Mr. Bergen. "Get out while you can"—get out of that mentality that there is a "right" way to live. (Well, technically there is, I believe it's called the Golden Rule, and you can find it either in the Bible or on a coffee mug, I forget.)

I know some people think that not wanting kids means I'm cold, but I'm not totally without baby urges. I felt something when I saw my friend Grace's baby all swaddled in a blanket on the couch. She looked like a yawning peanut. She was just a content little lump, drooling and going in and out of sleep. And I got that feeling deep down inside that almost brought tears to my eyes. I got an urge and I thought, *Oh my God. I want to . . .* be a baby.

1. Welcome Back, Kirkman

After graduating from Boston's Emerson College in June 1996 with a bachelor of fine arts in "theater arts," I moved back into my parents' house. (There are few to no well-paying jobs available to a girl who minored in rolling around on the floor collecting dust bunnies on her sweatpants—otherwise known as "modern dance.") I wish I'd had a really good reason for moving back home, like my friend Jayson from freshman year in college. It was rumored that Jayson took too much acid and also became possessed by the devil on the same night—this rumor started because he dropped two tabs while doing a séance around a pentagram that Mick, his practicing Satanist roommate, had burned into their dorm room rug. After the devil possessed him and/or the bad trip never wore off, folklore has it that Jayson was forever unable to speak but couldn't stop laughing—like some kind of demonic hyena. Jayson left school during his first semester and moved into his mom's basement, where he sat staring at the wall and listening to Pink Floyd's *Dark Side of the Moon* most of the day, except for the time he spent at his part-time job at his hometown library. I know that story sounds implausible—what library would employ a loud laugher?

Anyway, I didn't have an excuse for moving back home that I could pin on my mom and dad either, such as: it turned out that my mom wasn't just a hypochondriac and she actually did have a fatal heart murmur and it was her dying wish for me to move back into my childhood bedroom that was still covered with floral psychedelic wallpaper from the 1970s. That would have been a good one (except for the fatal heart murmur part).

It's not like I hadn't made plans for my postcollege life. I had. My plan was to become a famous television actress, the type who could play younger, because as a twenty-one-year-old, I still looked sixteen, just like everyone on *Beverly Hills 90210* (well, except for Andrea). Always a realist, I also had a backup plan and that was to become a famous actress on Broadway. I'd certainly put in some semiquality time training to be an actress. I spent every morning in acting class, putting my hand on my solar plexus to find my emotion and then breathing from my diaphragm. I usually found only a cough when I breathed deeply from my diaphragm because I'd developed a pack-a-day habit of smoking Camel Lights. I inhaled the acting class air like a young, hopeful girl, then hacked and wheezed out phlegm like a longshoreman whose emphysema gets exacerbated by his seasonal pneumonia.

I was convinced that simply because I attended college and majored in acting, I would walk out of the not-a-serious-acting-conservatory Emerson College and straight into my own trailer in Hollywood or some backstage door on Forty-second Street. The details were not mine to work out! That's what acting professors were for! This was before I realized that my acting professors were themselves actors who also thought at one point in their misguided youth that they'd be famous. I don't think any of them ever got offered a role in *The Godfather* and told Coppola, "Thanks for thinking of me, but I'm going to have to turn this role down. My real passion is to wake up every morning and teach a bunch of hungover college kids the concept of sense memory."

In all my years of college, I never really sat down and got to thinking, *Okay, so how do I take this class where I do monologues from* Equus *and turn it into a career?* I was usually busy thinking about the cute

Kurt Cobain look-alike who was always sitting alone in the cafeteria near the cereal. (Turns out that the reason he looked so much like Kurt Cobain was that he was also a heroin addict. I recently looked him up on Facebook and now he's a chubby, short-haired, button-up-shirt-wearing computer programmer—married, with two kids. I mourn this outcome more than if he had OD'd.)

In the back of my mind I just assumed that there existed a special red phone in the dean's office at Emerson. In my limited knowledge of how the world actually worked, I decided that this phone I made up in my head existed solely for placing and receiving calls to and from Hollywood. I pictured a kingmaker with a Santa Claus–esque workshop running Hollywood, who kept a master list. Instead of who's naughty and who's nice, his list had names of who's talented and who's not. I pictured my acting teacher calling this Hollywood Santa and saying something like, "Hi. This is Judith Renner. I'd like to report that Jen Kirkman just made herself cry in my Acting 101 class. Yes, she was doing a monologue about being a single mother but she used the image of her favorite dead pet as a catalyst for the tears. She was also speaking from her diaphragm and not mumbling. Oh, and she also nailed this really difficult Fosse dance move that involves crooking her pinky finger and sitting on a chair. Can we move her up on the 'talented' list? Great. We'll be in touch once she nails a Scottish accent—specifically the Shetland Isles."

A FEW WEEKS before I graduated from college, in lieu of a realistic life plan, I decided I'd get a life-altering haircut. I didn't even plan the haircut. It just came to me as I walked by a Supercuts. I went in, plopped into an empty chair, and told some girl to give me the "Mia Farrow in *Rosemary's Baby*" pixie cut. What I really wanted was the "Winona Ryder in *Reality Bites*" pixie cut, but I was too self-conscious to ask for that one. I'd always been told that I resembled Winona and I didn't want people to think that I was aware of that fact and trying to be like her. Of course, all I wanted was to be like her—mainly because she was dating Johnny Depp at the time and always got to play characters in movies that smoked cigarettes. Two things that thrilled me about the possibility of becoming an actor were (1) having an excuse to smoke if "my character" called for it and (2) doing love scenes with hot guys.

Within three minutes of walking into Supercuts, my hair was on the floor like a slut's thong and what was left of it was sticking straight up off the top of my head. The woman with the scissors said, "Whoops." Who knows whether she was even an actual employee. She could have been a sociopath off the street who carried scissors and wore a red-stained apron that she swore was just "hair dye." I looked stupid but I felt strangely liberated. I'd just done a really spontaneous thing that I could not take back or correct for a long time—sort of like getting pregnant or having an abortion. It gave me an immediate Zen acceptance of who I was.

Nevertheless, the haircut looked like shit, so I went down the street to a real salon where I had to confess to an about-to-combust gay guy that I'd been careless enough to trust Supercuts to get the *Rosemary's Baby/Reality Bites* pixie cut correct. He did a dramatic pinwheel with his arms and brought his fist to his chin like the statue *The Thinker*, then took a deep breath and placed his hands on my shoulders. He cried up to the ceiling, "Hon. What *are* we going to do?" Then he moved back and, with tears in his eyes, waved his hand in front of his face like a lady about to faint on her porch from either humidity or a sexy gentleman caller.

He took another deep breath.

"Hon, I have no choice but to nearly shave your head and leave a few pieces of bangs in the front. And you're going to have to act like you meant to do this. It's going to be very runway and you just have to promise me that you'll never wear this hairstyle without product or . . . an attitude."

I agreed—anything to get him to stop grabbing me so hard and behaving like he was a character from a Tennessee Williams play.

I went to a college party that night and when I climbed out the window onto the fire escape to smoke a cigarette, my favorite acting teacher was already sitting on the steps about to rip a bong hit. She exhaled a cloud of smoke in my face and said to me, "The hair. I like it. You're not hiding anymore. You're really you now, aren't ya, Jen? Aren't ya?" I had no idea what she meant, but I was still under the impression that she was going to pick up that red phone as soon as she was done getting high with a bunch of twenty-one-year-olds, to let Hollywood know that I was no longer hiding. I held out hope that something would save me from my credit card debt. I'd just added another couple of hundred bucks to my MasterCard to have that queen at the chichi salon shave my head.

I'D PASSED MY college years spending money on important things like tapestries for my bedroom walls and cigarettes for my lungs and now it was time to tighten my belt buckle—or at least to get a belt. The good thing about moving back home with my parents was that they weren't the type to try to teach me a lesson by charging me rent. They probably had more fun just silently judging me.

My original life plan had been to graduate and then move in with my boyfriend, Jamie. The only problem with that was that Jamie had dumped me a few months before graduation. (That also could have been a catalyst for the haircut, now that I think about it.) Jamie lived with his friends Adam and John, in the closet of Adam's bedroom. We'd lay in his single bed, watching his shirts hang above our heads, listening to Adam snore through the closet door and making plans for the day when Adam would move out and Jamie and I could take his room. When we weren't fumbling to get each other's pants off on a thin mattress on the floor of his closet, we were in the same college sketch comedy troupe called This Is Pathetic, which actually would have been a great label for our relationship.

Jamie and I were opposites. The only thing we had in common was our comedy troupe. Jamie was a beer-drinking, sports-loving fraternity guy. When I wanted to go see the Ramones play at a rock club in Boston on Valentine's Day, that was the beginning of our end. He didn't like the same music I did, yet he didn't want me running around to concerts by myself on such a Hallmark holiday. He said it "embarrassed him" that his woman attended a show alone. I never got the chance to ask him before he died, but I don't think Joey Ramone gave a shit that I went unaccompanied to see his band play.

Jamie always told me that I reminded him of his best friend from high school, Paula, for whom he'd always had unresolved feelings. He and I would take long, romantic walks through the Boston Common and he'd just stop and smile at me. He had a fantastic smile. He was like a shorter, greasier-faced Robert Downey Jr. I'd say, "Yes, Jamie?" waiting to hear him profess his love for me. And he'd say, "Sorry, you're just so . . . Paula right now," and then hug me tightly. I was too young to realize that if your boyfriend has feelings for his unrequited high school love and high school was only four years prior, you're not just a pleasant reminder of his youth; you're a Second-Place Paula.

Jamie dumped me after running into Paula when he went home for a weekend to visit his mother. He said they fell in love that weekend and it just "happened." As I type this I realize that he probably didn't "run into her" but had been talking to her all along, and his visit with his mother was really just his planned rendezvous with Paula. Oh my God, I was so stupid back then. But at least today I don't have lopsided boobs after two kids, like Paula does. Oh, and she didn't end up with Jamie. He was just a detour on her way to marrying a *different* guy from high school.

I'd just assumed that Jamie and I would be together all summer and our love would be my backup plan in case the getting-famous thing didn't happen right after graduation. I definitely didn't want to have kids with him—we were both professionally undiagnosed but in my opinion clinically depressed. Any offspring of ours would probably fight to stay in my womb because it would be too despondent and tormented to want to be born. I didn't necessarily want to get married to Jamie either; I just wanted to continue to be distracted by him. When he broke my heart, it felt like he stole my future or, alternatively, was making me face it. I was devastated and unable to get out of bed, like a mom, somewhat ironically, with an unfortunate case of postpartum depression.

I swore I would never love again until a few weeks later, when I went to a party and met a junior at Emerson named Blake. I know his name makes him sound like a rich kid from *Pretty in Pink* but he was actually the son of a single mom from a working-class town in Massachusetts, which is way more hot—it's like getting the dude from a John Cougar Mellencamp song who's going to make out with you in the back of his truck.

Blake was an actor (still is) and a damn good one. He was skinny and small with a slight underbite and watery blue eyes, and he dressed like he was wearing someone's hand-me-downs from the Partridge Family. One of my friends once told me that she thought that he looked like a mouse, but when Blake was onstage—he was a man. He touched off something in my DNA that craves and lusts after very skinny guys in bell-bottoms with 1970s-inspired shaggy haircuts. It probably has something to do with all of those full-color booklets inside the Led Zeppelin albums that my sister had in our bedroom. I love outgoing and gregarious men who want as much attention as I do. I've always had a thing for guys who make a living doing something in public (with the exception of someone who hands out sandwich shop flyers or dresses up like Pluto at Disney World).

Blake was the opposite of what I was faced with in my real life. He was a free spirit who stole cans of tuna fish from the grocery store while I was saddled with student loans, credit card debt, and the reality of moving back in with my parents. Blake spent his days wearing essential oils like Egyptian musk, reading books about the Stanislavsky acting method, and playing the drums, while I was gearing up to take a nine-to-five job in the sales department of the Boston Ballet.

Once I moved back in with my parents, I just assumed that it was tacitly understood that as a grown woman, I'd sleep over at Blake's apartment sometimes. It's not like he could come over and sleep with me. I had a single bed with wheels. One thrust and my bed would be on the other side of my room and my mom would probably yell, "You're scratching the floor up when you scrape the wheels against it like that, Jennifah!"

I'd assumed that four years of college had matured both my parents and me. I'd assumed that since I was twenty-one, there was no way they could think that I was still a virgin. (I mean, not that I think they sat around thinking about it. That would be creepy. Although I imagine if I were married and raising a teenage kid, their sex life would in fact be all I'd be able to think about. If I had a boy, I'd stop walking in his room unannounced once he turned eleven for fear that I'd catch him masturbating. If I had a teenage daughter, I imagine I'd sit there trying to watch TV at night but instead be wondering, *Is she out having sex right now?* Do husbands and wives have quiet nights at home when their teenagers aren't around and casually throw down, "How was your day, honey? Hey, do you think Susie has lost her virginity?")

My parents were very strict with me growing up. I wasn't allowed to have a telephone or a boy in my bedroom. If a boy happened to call me, I had to talk on the kitchen phone. My only hope for privacy was dragging the cord around the corner from the kitchen to crouch and whisper underneath our upright piano in the dining room. Sometimes I had to sneak into my parents' room to use their phone. That was even worse because the line would get staticky once my mom picked up the downstairs extension to eavesdrop. I don't know what she thought she was going to hear. When I was in high school, I had no idea what talking dirty was. The only earful my mom got was overhearing me nervously ask Adam the cute skateboarder, "Um, so, what's your favorite Cure song?"

During my senior year of college, I had lived in an off-campus apartment with two boys, Tim and David. It was like a reverse *Three's Company*, except unlike Jack Tripper, I didn't have to pretend to be gay in front of the landlord and I had no interest in seeing Tim or

David naked. They were like brothers to me. (I never had a brother, but I'm assuming it feels like having a male friend whom you don't want to bone.) When I told my very Catholic mother that I'd found somewhere to live . . . and it was with *two guys*, she said no right away. Actually she said more than no. What she said was, "Jennifah, the boys will rape you."

I don't think my mom quite understood the difference between a rapist and a male roommate. It's hard enough to share an apartment with a friend, because things can get pretty awkward if you owe him rent money. I can't imagine how delicate a situation it would be in the kitchen the morning after your roommate has forced himself on you.

Tim and David drove out to my parents' house in the suburbs to meet them, so that my mom could put faces to her daughter's future rapists' names. Their goofy demeanor and general innocent vibe won her over. She agreed to cosign the lease and let me move in with the guys who were such sweethahts—and I'm happy to say they never sexually violated me.

EVEN THOUGH I didn't think I had to ask permission to sleep at Blake's house now that I was a college graduate, it wasn't really a one-on-one, eye-contact-filled conversation that I wanted to have with my mom. I knew it would be awkward enough for her to see me leaving the house with an overnight bag. On my first night back, I finished unpacking and setting up my childhood bedroom to my liking and then turned right around to head into Boston to spend the night with Blake. I left a note on the kitchen table for my mom and dad—*Staying at Blake's tonight*—and hopped in my dad's spare Oldsmobile.

Blake and I were tangled up in his paisley sheets while Nag Champa incense burned in swirls around our heads, and my parents didn't know where Blake lived and had no way of contacting me. I think cell phones existed in 1996 but nobody I knew had one yet—if they did, it was in the form of a car phone with a long cord connected to the cigarette lighter. My folks never crossed my mind once. Why would I go home for the night? I'm an adult in the city and there's no need to drive home at two in the morning—and I have an irrational fear of getting in my car in the middle of the night and forgetting to check the backseat, only to be stuck on the road with a monster behind me, ready to strangle away. The next day, I walked in the front door and saw my mom sitting at the kitchen table. It was unusual for her to still be in her bathrobe at noon. That was her physical signal for "I'm so upset that I can't even get dressed." My mom sat there and flipped the pages of her newspaper very quickly, staring at me instead of the articles. I got the same feeling I used to get in my stomach when I was a little kid and I was in trouble. (Not that as a kid I ever got in trouble for sneaking out to sleep with my stoner boyfriend, but you know what I mean.) My mom said, "You didn't come home last night." I said, "I left a note." She said, "I know you did. Your father and I found it to be very bold." I said, "I have a boyfriend!"

And she said, "If you live under this roof, you live under my rules, and we do not allow sleeping over at a boyfriend's. If you want to be a trash bag, then you get your own house and behave like a trash bag there."

I'd never heard of being called a "trash bag" before, as opposed to just "trash." My mom was really throwing down. If we were the Real Housewives of Massachusetts, she would have ripped a crucifix off her neck and stabbed a hole in my Red Sox T-shirt. When I think about it, it's actually kind of a compliment, because my mom was implying that I'm strong, durable, and can be relied upon for clean up after a house party. I decided to respond like an adult, and since I didn't know how to be an adult, I got hysterical and stamped my feet. I slammed my fists on the creaky kitchen table and took a stand against living for free with my parents and driving their car. I screamed a few things about being in love and how they couldn't keep us apart. I grabbed the suitcase that I'd just unpacked the day before and started repacking. Had they not assumed I'd shared my bed with boys in college? Maybe they hadn't. When your daughter is in a sketch comedy troupe, maybe all you assume is that she isn't getting any.

At the last minute, I realized the Oldsmobile wasn't really *my* car and I'd have to walk with my stuffed suitcase to the commuter rail train that came once every three hours. *Fuck it*, I thought, and like a grown-up, I dragged my suitcase sans wheels down the street and a few flights of platform stairs, where I pouted and waited for a train heading to the city limits.

Blake lived in a part of Boston called Brookline Village, with three other guys. I figured what's one more person? When I arrived with my suitcase, his roommates were happy to see me and I went into Blake's room and immediately unpacked my things and hung them in his closet. While he was at class, I got all domestic, cleaned up his incense ashes, rinsed out his bong, and put his dirty clothes in the hamper. Later that night as we lay entwined on his futon, Blake asked, "So, have you thought about where you want to get an apartment?"

"Oh," I said, trying to conceal my disappointment, but it was hard to play it cool with a quivering lip and a bridal magazine in my hand.

Blake said, "I'm sorry, baby, but I can't have a live-in girlfriend my senior year in college." I ignored the fact that him calling me "baby" made me cringe. Sometimes Blake really thought he was a member of Earth, Wind & Fire. I told him that he needed to grow up. He came back at me with, "I'm not supposed to be grown up yet. You're twenty-one years old and a college graduate. You're the one who needs to grow up."

The next day, after Blake let me know that our committed relationship couldn't handle the extra commitment of permanently sharing his bed and his stolen cans of tuna, I went by myself to a party. My friend Zoey had just come back from New York City and was carrying around a copy of their free weekly newspaper the *Village*

Voice. There was an article about a new alternative comedy show on the Lower East Side called *Eating It* at a bar called the Luna Lounge. Although it wasn't a normal "comedy club," it was highly respected and a place where all of the coolest comedians went to try out new material. Getting up in front of people and just sort of talking had been something I'd wanted to explore ever since I was fifteen and I saw that episode of *Beverly Hills 90210* where Brenda Walsh started hanging out at a spoken-word open mic night at a coffee shop. She called herself a "hippie witch," moved out of her parents' house for a short stint, and sat on a stool, telling stories about high school.

I never went apartment hunting in Boston. After that party, I decided that becoming a stand-up comedian and getting my start in Manhattan was my destiny. If Blake thought that I should grow up and my parents thought that I wasn't adult enough to sleep at my boyfriend's house, I'd show everyone. I'd move to the toughest city in the world. I'd wanted to live in New York City ever since I saw my first black-and-white photo of James Dean smoking in a Manhattan diner. Sadly, I can't say that I've grown out of my urges to do things because I think that technically, if I were photographed doing them, it would make a really cool and iconic picture.

Even though the "plan" was to be a serious actress, I had always secretly wanted to be a stand-up comedian. It's safe to say I had about as much ambition and understanding of how to actually become a stand-up comedian as my mom had of how to become a high-priced call girl. But that article in the *Village Voice* seemed like it was written specifically for me to see. The closest I had come to doing comedy since This Is Pathetic was becoming a member of a local Boston improv group. (Improvisation—that fine art where a group of people stand onstage with nothing prepared and one of them asks the audience for a suggestion like an occupation or a location and someone inevitably shouts out, "Rectal exam!") I enjoyed messing around onstage and making people laugh, but I wasn't great at playing with others. It's not that I don't enjoy sharing the spotlight—I just don't like having to be responsible for other people.

Improv is all about supporting your teammates. (By the way, I hate when anything other than a professional sports team refers to itself as a "team." It has this air of forced camaraderie that has always made me uncomfortable, along with people who talk in baby voices to babies and to adults during sex.) Improv is similar to war in that you're expected to do anything to save the life of your partner. And as with war, people don't really understand what improv is "good for."

Improv requires one thing I lack that I think all mothers need—that basic instinct to put someone else first. I can barely forgive myself for the time when I negged Billy from my improv troupe onstage. He said, "I have a gift for you," and my first instinct was to say, "No you don't." The scene died right then and there. See what happens when I try to nurture something? I know it seems dramatic to relate destroying an improv scene to possibly destroying a child's life, but improv and child rearing are not so different. Both are jobs that people volunteer for and complain about endlessly, and they bore everyone around them as they talk about the process.

I broke the news to Blake that I was moving. He was surprised, since only twenty-four hours earlier I'd wanted to settle down and play house. I explained to him that if I wanted to do something as drastic as become a stand-up comedian, I had to really make a bold move and change cities. I couldn't become a new person in my old hometown. Blake agreed. He always agreed with me when I spoke excitedly and loudly about something—even if I was talking out of my ass.

My parents had changed the locks on me after I decided to leave them and attempt to move in with Blake. I never understood their reasoning for that move. Wouldn't that only ensure that I'd spend even more nights having patchouli-scented sex with my boyfriend at his off-campus apartment? I had to arrange a time so they could let me into my own bedroom to get the rest of my things. Blake was in the driveway, hiding from my folks and manning the small U-Haul truck that I'd rented to get me to Brooklyn, where I was going to live with my old college friends Amy and Ed. I didn't even have any furniture, just a couple of lamps and a wicker nightstand. The inside of our U-Haul looked like a Pier 1 had been renovated by a crackhead.

As ballsy as it may have been to move to Brooklyn without knowing anything about it—except what I'd seen in the opening credits of *Welcome Back, Kotter* as a kid—I was still a wimp in a lot of ways. I knew I had my parents' love but I wanted their approval. I couldn't bring myself to tell my mom and dad that my reason for moving to New York City was that I wanted to be a stand-up comedian. They never said point-blank, "Don't become a stand-up comedian," but I think that's an implied desire that parents have for their child from the moment he or she is born. That and "Don't become a stripper or a junkie, or a musician."

Being a comic is even harder than being in a band. A stand-up comedian wanders cities alone, saying dirty things into germ-ridden microphones to drunk people, whereas a musician sings things into a germ-ridden microphone to drunk people who at least want to give them free drugs and sleep with them after. So for the time being, I just told them that I was moving to New York City to get another job in some kind of box office and to start going on auditions as an actress—really put that BFA in theater arts to work.

In the front seat of the U-Haul Blake and I discussed our relationship. We wanted to remain a couple and try to do the long-distance thing. We agreed that we were only a four-hour train ride apart and it would be even more exciting when we saw each other. Right outside of the Bronx, I had to pee really badly, but the highway was basically a parking lot. The traffic wasn't going to move for a while, so I took a Snapple bottle, pulled my pants down, and squatted. I missed and peed on the floor of the van and on Blake's sneaker. Jewish people step on a glass after they take a vow, and in our fucked-up way, we sealed a long-distance relationship deal with my urine on Blake's foot.

Blake helped me carry my suitcases up the narrow staircase to my new third-floor walk-up in Brooklyn. My roommates weren't home but they'd left a key under the mat and a welcome note. When I saw my bedroom for the first time, it felt more like a giant fuck-you note. The room was so small that there was only space for a single bed and a small nighttable—which had to sit on the other side of the room if I ever wanted the door to open. I moved from living under my parents' restrictions to a room that physically restricted me from having any space to invite a boy to sleep over unless I moved my bedside table into the living room.

Blake had to get back to Boston to return the U-Haul before we were charged for an extra day. Before he left, he sat on my bed with me. He held me and we cried. The mutual tears seemed romantic, but the truth was that I was mourning my jail-cell-size bedroom and Blake was probably coming to grips with the fact that he had a four-hour drive in a van that reeked of fresh urine.

That night, I went by myself to a comedy show at a swanky club called Fez. I already had an intellectual inkling of becoming a co-median, but watching it live onstage—I got what can only be called an urge. I couldn't just sit there like a normal audience member. I wanted to get out of my seat and run up on the stage and just start talking. I wanted to wave to the audience members and say, "I'm one of them! Not you!" The pull was strong. I had to do this com-edy thing and I wanted to do it at the expense of everything else and I wanted to start right away. This was my proverbial moment of ovu-lation and I wanted to lie down on the ground with a pillow under my butt and let comedy just come inside me, and one day it would blossom and grow into a career baby.

I was disturbed from my sleep later that night by the loud noise. Yes, I lived over the Brooklyn-Queens Expressway, but the screeching that roused me wasn't the cars; it was my roommates having a fight. Did I mention that Amy and Ed were a couple? It was like living with my parents all over again. Amy had always been volatile in college, but I couldn't understand what there was to yell about once you'd moved in with a guy. So far, in my limited life experience, the yell-ing happened because the guy *wouldn't* move in with you. But now

Amy was upset at Ed because she wanted marriage and kids and was wondering why their cohabitation hadn't brought out that urge in him yet.

I understood her urge—not to get married and have kids but to have the life you envisioned for yourself. To fill up that pit in the gut that just says, "Gimme, gimme what I want. I promise I'll be good if you just gimme what I want!" That's how I felt about stand-up comedy. And if anyone had told me that I couldn't have it, I would've been yelling too. Although I related to Amy's feelings of longing, falling asleep to them was not soothing. I opened my window so that the sounds of the Mack trucks would drown out the sounds of the train wreck in their bedroom.

The next morning, I got on the Manhattan-bound F train after being laughed at by Amy for asking whether it was safe to carry a purse into New York City. I got off at Second Avenue and found my way to my mecca—the Luna Lounge. It was empty and I went up and confidently said to the bartender, "I want to perform at the alternative comedy show I read about in the *Village Voice*."

He shrugged. "I don't book it. You have to send a tape."

I was confused. "A tape of what?"

"A tape of you doing stand-up."

Now I was indignant. "But I have never done stand-up. I don't have a tape yet. I'm trying to start so I want to start here."

We went back and forth for a while—as I tried to convince him that I just knew I was funny and he tried to convince me that he had no power to get me on that stage. Imagine going to a job interview, refusing to bring a résumé or any references, and wanting to get hired on the promise that you'll do a really, really good job if they'd just hire you. I sat down at the bar, defeated. But then I realized, *Hey, I'm an adult. In New York City. I can have a drink in the daytime if I want* and *smoke a cigarette.* I ordered a beer and bummed a Merit Ultra Light off the bartender. I posed for the imaginary camera that was taking my James Dean–esque photo. I'd gotten what I wanted out of New York City and after only four days, I knew it was time to go home.

• • •

BACK IN BOSTON, things felt weird with Blake. I couldn't believe that four whole days spent in a long-distance relationship hadn't made him change his mind about not wanting to live with me. He said I could stay with him until I found an apartment. I did find an apartment. His apartment. And like a lost puppy, I stayed for almost a year. I got my old job back at the Boston Ballet and my old position back on the "team" at Improv Boston. I was disheartened at the thought of starting a stand-up career because it seemed like you couldn't start until you had already started and put it on tape. So I postponed that dream and focused on being Blake's clingy girlfriend.

As the months passed, the only thing tangled up in Blake's sheets was Blake. I was on the other side of the futon, shivering, struggling to get under the covers with him. Blake had made a new friend in his acting class, a female friend. She was starring in the college production of *The Diary of Anne Frank*. Blake lit up when he talked about her, and he talked about her a lot. He also talked *to* her a lot, on the phone, in his room, while I sat on his bed, watching. I got drunk one night at a party and confronted him in front of God and a kitchenful of his peers and screamed, "Are you fucking her?" He wasn't fucking her—until his girlfriend got drunk and crazy and screamed, "Are you fucking her?" And then that night, I'm pretty sure he fucked her, because he didn't come home. The next day we broke up.

I know it's wrong, and if I end up going to hell and meeting Adolf Hitler, I promise that I will kill him with my bare hands, but to this day when someone brings up *The Diary of Anne Frank*, I can't help but think to myself, *That little whore*.

My relationship with my parents had improved over that year. Somehow living with Blake wasn't as abhorrent to my folks as spending the night with Blake and then coming home the next morning in the same clothes in which I'd left their house—to see my boyfriend, who was planning to take those clothes right off. My mom and I sat at the kitchen table, where she'd referred to me as a "trash bag" just a year before. We were having our first frank discussion about sex, without actually talking about sex. Actually, we'd talked about sex once—in 1985.

In fifth-grade sex ed class, my teacher taught us what happens when sperm enters a woman's fallopian tubes. Our homework assignment was to draw a picture of the opposite sex—or what we thought the opposite sex looked like naked. Then we were to write a paragraph underneath, from our best understanding, of what intercourse was and how babies were made. I told my mom about the homework assignment and she teased me by chasing me around the kitchen table, asking to see what I'd drawn. I remember feeling disappointed in sex ed class. I'd had a vague inkling that sex was something that people did for fun, but the way it was being taught, it seemed like the teacher was dismissing that notion and instead presenting sex as something that two people do only when they want to make a baby. I half listened to the teacher explain how sperm meets egg, figuring, *I don't need to know this. I don't think I'm having kids anytime soon.*

I think about raising kids now and how they'd have access to Facebook and actual real pictures of naked people on the Internet. I think about how my ten-year-old daughter would be nothing like me. I had no idea what a penis looked like, so that picture I had to draw in fifth grade of a naked man looked like a Ken doll—just legs with no anatomy in between. My ten-year-old daughter probably would already have had a dick-pic sent to her cell phone by some little shit in her class. Would my ten-year-old daughter have to have a cell phone? I guess I could forbid her from having one—just like my mom forbade me from watching MTV because she thought music videos were too sexually explicit and directed by the devil. But then again, what if my daughter had to make an emergency call? There aren't pay phones on every corner these days. If some creep in a van were to abduct her outside of school, my daughter wouldn't be able to speed-dial 911 or text me. I can't send a ten-year-old girl to school with no viable means of communication. And what if my ten-year-old girl was an early bloomer and had her period already? Would I have to teach her about safe sex or secretly slip a birth control pill into her oatmeal every morning? I know that when I was ten I was terribly horny for Bruce Willis and Michael J. Fox. Luckily, the boys at school whom I liked didn't like me back, so my lust remained only a fantasy reserved for the hours that *Moonlighting* and *Family Ties* aired. But what about my imaginary daughter? What if the boys liked her back? Then they'd be screwing at my house after school while I was on tour doing comedy, and before you know it, I'd have a pregnant ten-year-old daughter and I'd be a grandmother *and* a mother to two people before one of them even turned eleven.

I don't understand what's so great about having kids when I'm faced with the fact that at some point my kids would disappoint me—just like I disappointed my parents. It's the vicious cycle of life. It's an absolute certainty that the babies that I'm not having would become horny teens who send pictures of their genitalia to one another on cell phones that I'm paying for.

Eleven years later, I sat around that same kitchen table with my mom as she gave her version of a mea culpa. "Jennifah, I'm reading a biography on Lauren Bacall. She had a lot of men in her life but she loved them deeply because she was passionate . . . about everything she did. She was a wond-ah-ful woman who was very talented."

That was my mom's way of telling me that I was forgiven and that even though she'd never slept with a man before marriage, it was something that "the kids" and Hollywood legends were doing and maybe it wasn't so abnormal or trash bag–like after all.

She'll never admit it, but I believe that my Catholic-but-starstruck mom gives a free pass to people in Hollywood on certain moral issues. The affair between JFK and Marilyn Monroe was blessed by my mom in ways that Monica Lewinsky and Bill Clinton's affair wasn't—and they only had oral/cigar sex! But Bill Clinton's saxophone-playing appearance on Arsenio Hall was not enough for my mother to consider him Hollywood royalty. My mom doesn't condone abusing prescription drugs, but to her, Judy Garland is a saint and a victim. She'll forever blame the movie studios for handing Judy the pills. And I remember when her best friend called to say that John Lennon had been shot—my mom said over the phone, "Oh Ruthie. It's just not fair. A Beatle shouldn't be allowed to die."

As long as my mom and I were having a heart-to-heart, I summoned up the rest of my gumption and told her that I wanted to be a stand-up comedian. I knew I was killing her dream of my owning my own little local dance studio or becoming a Broadway actress. Her response was, "Are you even funny? You are very dramatic, Jennifah." I reminded her of how I'd always wanted to be voted class clown in the Pollard Middle School yearbook. (By the way, "class clown" seemed to be the moniker given to the most humorless and bullying jocks. What class clown really means is "most popular"; the kids who grow up to be truly funny are shoved into lockers.)

AGAINST MY MOM'S wishes, I continued the pursuit of stand-up comedy, but I did live in my childhood bedroom, with no male visitors, like a good, celibate twenty-two-year-old girl. Every night I clicked and clacked on the Kirkman family word processor, attempting to write jokes.

One of my first jokes was about Nancy Reagan's "Just Say No" campaign from the 1980s. I have no idea why that was still on my mind in the 1990s. The joke was horrible. It wasn't even a joke. It wasn't even a complete thought. It went something like this: "Nancy Reagan says to 'just say no'—well, I say that's not realistic. I think you should 'just say maybe,' and then try to walk away from the drugs. It doesn't make you look like a dork who says no. It just looks like you have something else to do."

I thought that joke would immediately cement me in the pantheon of great edgy political comedians who also comment on the sociology of humanity—like Richard Pryor or George Carlin. I started to read it to my mom and she just looked at me. She put her head in her hands, much like that gay hairdresser who'd had to shave my head. "Oh, Jennifah. That just isn't funny." I rolled my eyes and said, "Mom, you just don't get it." I stormed out of the house and got in the trusty white Oldsmobile and struck out for Cambridge, Massachusetts, and my first open mic in the back of a bar at the Green Street Grill. I was headed for my Brenda Walsh moment.

I swilled a few cheap glasses of merlot before I sat down on the stool onstage at the open mic. I drew a breath and got ready to tell my Nancy Reagan joke. I looked out at a bunch of people my age, waiting expectantly, actually listening before I'd even said anything. I could hear my mom's voice: "Jennifah, that just isn't funny." I made myself laugh as I thought about my poor mom sitting in her recliner, tens of thousands of dollars poorer because she'd spent her life buying food, faux designer clothes, and cassette tapes for my two sisters and me, and this was how I was repaying her.

It made me laugh out loud. So I skipped my Nancy Reagan joke and I just told the audience that I was a college graduate who lived with my parents and my mother did not think I was funny. And then I started to impersonate my mom. I'd been imitating her since I was a kid around the house—but until now it never dawned on me to impersonate my mom in front of strangers. It was always more of an in-joke with my family.

I killed. I'm not bragging. All comedians do really well the first time they do stand-up comedy. I don't know what it is—some cosmic/karmic free pass because what you're doing is hard enough. But when you're just starting out, you don't know that all comics kill their first time—that's why we stay comics. We think we're special.

A few months later, my parents came to see me perform. Let's just say there was another kitchen-table discussion—this time with my mom in tears. She didn't understand why I was humiliating her in public and revealing family secrets. I tried to convince my mom that making jokes about how she pretends she's not home when the annoying neighbor knocks on the door is not a "family secret." My parents didn't come back to see me perform and things were definitely strained until my mother saw the Margaret Cho movie *I'm the One That I Want*. Margaret had proven herself to be a successful and famous comedian who also imitated her mother. Just like she came to accept Lauren Bacall's sex life, she saw via Margaret's documentary that comedians are actually honoring the ones they love when they make fun of them in their act. My mother not only gave me her seal of approval but also started to come to see me perform regularly so that she could watch the audiences laugh at . . . *her*. And just like Margaret's mom, mine stuck around after the show to get attention from the crowds.

MY MOM HAS a really good singing voice. She's part of a singing group—you may have heard of them, they're called the Musettes. Oh, you haven't heard of them? That's probably because you don't live in a senior citizens' home. That's where they tour. My mom plays piano and sings with three other women and leads them in a rousing (for those settled-down seniors) rendition of "Oh, We Ain't Got a Barrel of Money."

One of my mom's favorite stories is that when she was a teenager she met Patti Page. I'll spare anyone under forty who is reading this book the trip to Wikipedia. Patti Page is one of the biggest-selling female recording artists in history. She's famous for songs like "Old Cape Cod" and "Mockin' Bird Hill." When my mom met Patti Page she told her that she wanted to be a singer like her someday, and Patti said to her, "You can be anything you want to be."

That story always depressed me because by the time my mom relayed Patti's words to me, I knew how it ended. Sure, my mom could have been anything she wanted to be, but she didn't become a professional, Grammy-winning, popular American singer. Instead, she had three kids and raised them in a time when you couldn't really just strap your kid into a stroller and pursue your dream of becoming a singer. *American Idol* hadn't been invented yet.

I can't imagine dreaming of wanting to be a singer, meeting my idol, and getting her words of encouragement—and then getting married, having kids, and touring the blue-hair circuit. Luckily, my mom raised me using Patti Page's insight "You can be anything you want to be," and not "You can be anything you want to be but it probably won't work out that way" or "You can be anything you want to be but also please still make time to be a mother and wife."

Some of her friends have accused her of living vicariously through my show business life. I don't see it that way. She's definitely not a stage mother. My mom just always knew how much my career meant to me and she's a realist. She doesn't just blindly say, "You can have it all!"

Life is like a closet full of clothes—you *can* have it all, but it doesn't mean that you should. I *can* wear four cardigan sweaters all at once with a pair of sweatpants over my jeans—but it doesn't mean that I *should*.

I credit my mom with giving me the delusional level of confidence I needed to think that I could actually make a living in show business. For example, she resented that in order to get accepted as a theater major at Emerson, I had to audition. She walked into the dean's office, VHS tape in hand, and said, "Here is a tape of Jennifah. She played Bonnie in *Anything Goes* in the high school musical. She can tap-dance, act, and sing and you want her to do two contrasting monologues for you to get into this college?"

To be fair, I don't think my mom's unrealized dreams of becoming a singer plagued her the way that I have to assume I'd be plagued if I weren't earning a living and continuing to pursue a life in the world of comedy. Back in my mom's world, in Massachusetts in 1950-something, you could have a dream but you understood your reality, which was that the nice guy named Ronnie from high school wanted to marry you and your father approved of him and so you went to secretarial school during the engagement. Once married, it was time to start making those babies. It's amazing to me that my parents have been married for over fifty years. They were high school sweethearts. I was raised by two people who, because they were getting along so well in homeroom, decided to get married and make other people.

If I'd married my high school sweetheart—well, there was more than one—but if I'd married the one who inspired me to write poems in my diary, I'd now be living with him in his mom's basement. (Before you judge, he does have a job and he pays his mom rent. So he's got one foot in the real world and he's now bald— which gives him the appearance of being very wise.)

Anyway, pretty soon someone else besides my mom started to sneak around my comedy shows. Blake was back. I think he was mostly curious that I hadn't called him in months, begging him to leave Anne in her attic and come back to me. We had one last one-night stand after one of my gigs. He was a college graduate at this point and he was even paying for his own tuna fish. He told me he wanted to move somewhere like Los Angeles to become an actor but he also wanted to retire young, move back to Boston to live near his family, be a sports announcer for the Red Sox, and . . . have kids. I felt uncomfortable in Blake's bed after he said that—and that wasn't just because his worn-out futon mattress made me feel like I was sleeping on the bench of a dry sauna. Some instinct was rolling around inside of me—I didn't want to be the woman to give Blake children.

I remembered that when we were dating, Blake would call his three-year-old nephew and talk to him like he was an adult. He'd ask, "Hey, buddy, are you lookin' smooth today?" It always seemed so foreign to me that Blake was so good with children. It made me uncomfortable. I told one of my girlfriends about it at the time and she laughed and said, "Jen, you should be so happy that he's going to be a good father!" Then she armchair-analyzed me and said that I was just jealous of the attention that Blake was giving his nephew, that we were newly in love and I wanted him all to myself.

I was so attracted to my feathered-haired ex-boyfriend that I was tempted to beg him to get back together with me. But I could not unknow what I knew. He wanted different things for his future than

I did. Blake didn't seem like such a free spirit to me anymore. The guy who rolled over in the morning and relit a joint before breakfast . . . wanted to be a father? And he was already sure of that? I tried to picture myself pregnant in our kitchen together. I had no ability to envision a future where it even seemed possible that I'd want a baby. It made me want to cross my legs and board up my vagina.

I mourned Blake for months but I stuck with the comedy. Eventually things started looking up. After twenty-two years, my mom finally let me install my very own private landline with a separate phone number in my bedroom. There was nothing to eavesdrop on anymore—I was letting it all hang out and doing just what Patti Page had advised. I was being whatever I wanted to be. And let me tell you, the other silver lining is that for a girl who doesn't want babies, living with your parents in your early twenties is the best free birth control around.

2. Misadventures in Babysitting

Most of my friends who have kids insist that they won't make the same mistakes their parents made. They read books and take classes. My friend Shannon is on a one-woman personal crusade via Facebook updates to get all toxic toys off the market. She's not going to let her baby put plastic products in his mouth like she did. My friend Tracy doesn't say no in a stern voice to her toddler. Instead, when he goes toward a light socket with his wet finger, she stops him and asks, "Is that the right choice?" (And it works!) Maybe we can prevent our kids from hating us for the same reasons that we hated our parents, but I have a feeling that they'll just end up hating us for a whole new set of reasons—which is why I want no part of this cycle.

I'm the youngest out of three girls in my family. There's this myth out there that parents are pretty lenient with their youngest kid. I always heard things like "Oh, by the time I came around my parents loosened up. When I was a kid I didn't have a bedtime. I didn't even have a bedroom. I had my own apartment down the street from my parents." Not me. My parents were the most strict with me, their innocent theater-geek baby girl whose only real desire in life was to wear all black and star in Needham High School's version of *The Crucible*.

The restrictions placed on my teenage life read like a really fucked-up rule board:

- No boyfriends allowed! It's not called date rape for nothing!
- Talking to a boy on the phone is allowed only during daylight hours and in a room where you can't shut the door! And *no whispering*!
- If you go to Dunkin' Donuts instead of church on Sundays—you're not fooling God! That's an automatic purgatory sentence!
- Diaries will be randomly searched! You shouldn't be writing about secrets anyway!
- You can only go to your friends' houses at night when a parent is home. Even then I'm not happy about it because your friends' mothers are pushovers!
- Sleepovers at girlfriends' houses are strictly forbidden! Are you really just "sleeping"?
- Curfew is at 10:30 p.m.! No exceptions. Except to come home earlier.
- No driving a car unless one of your parents is in the front seat. And even then—where do you think you're going?

Once I'd successfully survived my teen years by following their foolproof guidelines, my mom sent me to college, having saved every penny she'd earned. Her dad had told her that women didn't go to college, so she and all the other moms of her generation raised their daughters to aspire to college. And I think my mom telling me not to be so boy-crazy was more than a subtle hint that the priorities of a new era of women were emerging (that and she really didn't want me to end up enduring a teenage pregnancy).

But each generation makes new mistakes. For example, I know that I wouldn't feed the son that I'm never going to have white bread or processed cheese, but I wouldn't have the answer if he couldn't sleep and called out to me in the night, "Mommy, Mommy, there's a monster under my bed!" I believe in monsters and if he were telling me that in the next room there was a monster on the loose? I'd yell back, "Of course there's a monster under your bed, honey, that's where they live!"

I've *already tried* to influence kids by doing things differently than my parents and I'll tell you right now, it didn't work. Most Saturday nights from 1988 to 1992, you could find me at the Reinhardts' house, babysitting their four-year-old son, Eli. I fell into babysitting for Eli through a friend. I substituted for Eileen one day and after that fateful afternoon, Eli started saying, "Don't want Eileen. Want Jen to play." And from then on, my Saturday nights belonged to a four-year-old. That was the only time I ever stole a man from another woman.

I still think it's weird that adults would leave a toddler with a fourteen-year-old, whom they barely know, especially in a house filled with sharp-edged glass coffee tables. It makes me feel old, like I grew up in some kind of 1940s *It's a Wonderful Life* world where everyone knew one another and Eli wasn't in any real danger because an angel was watching our every move and the townspeople would come over with baskets of money in case of emergency.

When I interviewed with Mr. Reinhardt for the position of babysitter (or, what I think is a more accurate job description, "Person in Charge of Making Sure Someone's Kids Don't Die While They're Out Seeing a Movie"), he asked me, "So, do you like kids?" I was stumped. Like kids? I never thought about kids. I was the youngest and basically an only child. I didn't have any experience in playing with kids younger than I was. I don't even remember playing well with others when I *was* a kid. My friends enjoyed things like sledding, which involved too much prep for my taste, plus putting on long underwear, a few more layers over that, and a big, puffy Michelin Man coat—only to have snow find its way into your sock. I hate being cold and spending ten minutes walking up a snowbank just to spend two seconds sliding down. I always wanted to skip to the good part—going back inside, having hot chocolate, and watching Richard Dawson host *Family Feud*.

"Name something that most kids like doing, except for little Jen Kirkman. Survey says? Having fun!"

I didn't know what to tell Mr. Reinhardt. I didn't *hate* kids. I just never thought about them. Kids evoked an "eh" emotion in me at best. But I wasn't going to make eight dollars an hour sitting at home with my parents on a Saturday night, so I told my first but most definitely not my last white lie on the subject: "Yes. I love kids. I'm great with them."

Babysitting every Saturday night felt like the world's most boring New Year's Eve, as I sat there counting down the last hour before little Eli's bedtime. One night Eli couldn't sleep. He was talking as if he'd been reading a Nietzsche pop-up book. Right before I was about to turn out the light he asked, "Jen? Is there a God?"

Me: "Well, what does your mom say about God?"
Eli: "I never asked her. I just thought of it."
Me: "Why don't you wait and ask your mom about God in the morning? She has all the answers."
Eli: "I thought all grown-ups knew. You're a grown-up!"

If only he knew that even though I was in charge, I was just a kid myself. I hadn't even had my first real kiss yet. I was wearing an A-cup bra. Really it was a training bra. There were no cups. It was almost like wearing an Ace bandage around my upper torso. I was so *not* a grown-up.

Eli persisted. "If God can see me, why can't I see him?" (A Jewish kid wanted a Catholic girl to explain to him why we can't see God. Oy boy!) Then he started to get hysterical: "I don't want God watching me sleep!"

I had no idea how to answer Eli. I didn't know the first thing about the Jewish God. I knew that Jesus was Jewish and that Moses . . . did some . . . stuff. I'm not even sure of the timeline. I couldn't remember whether those guys knew each other or whether they just sort of respected each other's "miracle corners."

When I was a little older than Eli was then, my mom tucked me in every night and we said that prayer: "If I die before I wake, I pray the Lord my soul to take." That prayer is comforting—if you're ninety and on a respirator. It doesn't make much sense for a healthy eight-year-old. Then, after we prayed about this Lord guy coming to take me away in my sleep, my mom would shut the light off and close the door, leaving me to stew in my newly developed neurosis. I couldn't do the same thing to Eli.

Standing in Eli's doorway, looking at his innocent little face, I didn't have the heart to just turn the light out and ignore him. I wouldn't have to wait until I had my own kids. This was my moment to make an impact on the youth of America by doing the exact opposite thing that my parents did. I would not tell him that there is a God waiting to take him in his sleep.

While I racked my brain for the best way to answer his question without really answering his question, Eli, in the manner of children everywhere with too much time on their hands, came up with more questions. Such as, "When am I gonna die?"

I knew I had to protect him and let him remain a kid. Kids need myths, like the tooth fairy, and when they're older they can handle the truth: that your parents flush your teeth down the toilet like they're getting rid of forensic evidence and leave you only twenty-five cents, not accounting for the inflation that's occurred since they were kids. You'll have to borrow a dollar from them later anyway in order to afford a Charleston Chew candy bar and they'll guilt you and say, "That will pull your teeth out." By the time Eli knew the truth about anything I'd be in college and wouldn't have to worry about helping him process it. For tonight, in order to protect him and get myself out of his room and on to the bag of Oreos waiting for me in the Reinhardts' kitchen, I would *lie my ass off.*

"Oh, Eli," I said. "You will live to be two hundred years old before you die and that is a very, very long time from now."

I was proud of myself until Eli said, "So, I am going to die?"

I said, "No. No. I mean, *if* you die, you will die at two hundred, but . . . not everybody dies."

Eli said, "So, some people die and some don't?"

Um. Yes.

Eli said, "Why did God make my grandpa die?"

Um . . .

Eli asked, "Can I die before I turn two hundred if I'm murdered in my bed?"

I'm glad that I didn't think to raid the Reinhardts' medicine cabinet to see whether the missus had any "mother's little helper," because I seriously would have considered crushing some into the orange juice on Eli's nightstand to help him take his mind off bed-murder.

Fuuuck. How did this kid know about murder? He's right. Murder is scary. And it's real, even in seemingly safe havens like Needham, Massachusetts. Some guy in our town had chopped his wife into tiny pieces in their bathtub just streets away from where little Eli Reinhardt lived. I was terrified of murder myself and to be honest I didn't like the idea of the Reinhardts' glass sliding doors in their living room. Sure, they had locks, but I could just picture the murderer tossing his ax through the thin glass, shattering it, and then walking purposefully toward me with a bloodthirsty gleam in his eye. "But I don't even really live here!" I'd scream. As if that would be a good reason why he shouldn't introduce me to the pointy end of his ax.

I still had a chance to be a good substitute parent. I told Eli that there was no such thing as murder. I told him it was just a thing he saw on TV but not actually something that was physically possible. People couldn't kill other people, so he had nothing to worry about.

As a special treat, I decided to lie on the floor next to Eli's bed. I told him that I'd lie there until he fell asleep so that if he had any more scary thoughts, I'd be right there. Once Eli was asleep and dreaming of a vengeful God, I snuck out, whipped the blinds shut in the living room, and stuffed my face with Oreos.

I had no idea that kids under the age of five had the capacity to remember things from week to week. I thought Eli would have forgotten all about murder and dying at age two hundred by the time I saw him seven days later. Nope. Eli wanted me to sleep on his floor again, and as I lay there he worried out loud that his parents would get murdered. He asked, "If my parents were murdered, would you live here and take care of me?"

How did I go from favorite babysitter to guardian-in-case-of-a-double-homicide? I reinstated my lie to Eli. "Eli, no one is getting murdered. I told you. It's not real."

Should I tell the Reinhardts about Eli's obsession with untimely death? I couldn't tell them that I fell asleep on his floor—that would make me sound like some kind of perv. I felt like I'd fucked this kid up for life. Maybe there's something parents know that babysitters don't—like how to properly and with authority squelch all conversations about stabbings and how to not do what the kid wants just so you can get what *you* want, because eventually that type of negotiation brings everyone down.

A few weeks later Mrs. Reinhardt talked to me woman-to-teenager about the little boy we were raising. She was distraught because Eli kept saying that he wanted to stab people to see whether they would die. Ever since I told Eli there was no such thing as murder, he had apparently gotten confused and become sort of obsessed with this crime. She said that Eli was mad at God for picking his grandfather to die. She asked me, "Jennifer, why was he thinking about such things? How did these ideas get put in Eli's head?"

I don't know, Mrs. Reinhardt. Chalk it up to . . . kids *think* the darndest things?

The Reinhardts eventually stopped calling me. I'm sure that wasn't Eli's decision—after all, I was to be his godmother after his parents were found bludgeoned in their beds by the Massachusetts Murderer.

I ATTEMPTED BABYSITTING one more time with the Roberts family. The Robertses also had a four-year-old son; his name was Danny. I actually looked forward to spending time with little Danny. He didn't have the dark streak that Eli did.

I never had to worry about getting Danny to go to sleep or

explaining that one day when he was two hundred years old his heart would stop beating, because I only babysat Danny on weekday afternoons. Danny didn't force his kid-agenda on me. Sure, he made me watch *Mac and Me* (the poor man's *E.T.*) a few times but he'd often hand me the remote and say, "You pick." So I picked. And Danny and I spent many afternoons together watching the video for "Fascination Street" by the Cure on MTV. I had a crush on Robert Smith, the lipsticked lead singer. Danny would tease me and say, "He's your *boyyyfriend.*"

A few weeks into this gig, I was stuffing my face with ice cream and I lost sight of Danny for a few minutes. He showed up in the kitchen with red lipstick smeared on his face. He announced, "I like Mommy's makeup." I sprang to action and started wiping Revlon no. 2 off Danny's face. That's when he announced, "Jennifer, I want to French-kiss boys."

Well, at least he didn't want to murder anybody.

Danny's mom came home and I had to explain to her that Danny didn't have a rash on his mouth. It was a stain—from this season's hottest matte lipstick color.

She was upset that I'd turned my back for a minute, something I guess you can't do when a little boy with a makeup fetish is running around the house.

As she drove me home she said, "I've been meaning to talk to you anyway, Jennifer. You can't have boys over when you babysit Danny. He can't stop talking about your boyfriend Robert Smith."

After turning Danny into a future drag queen, I took a self-imposed leave of absence from the babysitting business. I'd learned that you couldn't talk to kids about death or show them music videos of men who sing in eyeliner. I possibly had turned one kid into an obsessive-compulsive with the urge to murder, and another kid gay. I'm not equating being a murderer with being gay, but from what I understand, either can be a difficult thing to admit to your family.

3. Toddlers Without Borders

Sitting on my coffee table are *Vanity Fair* magazines dating back to December 2010 that I haven't had a chance to read yet. My DVR is full of *Real Time with Bill Maher* episodes from the 2012 election that I'll get around to watching by the 2016 election, I'm sure. I do not know where all of this "spare time" is that people who have kids always tell me I have.

I'm also totally ADHD. Yes, it's a real disease, but I admit that "totally ADHD" is not a real medical term. I have an actual hyperactivity disorder and that's why when I drink coffee, I get sleepy. I got excited when my doctor gave me a prescription for an ADHD medication that can make you feel jumpy and lose weight. The catch is that you only get jumpy and lose weight if you abuse the medication. When you take ADHD medication as needed, you just feel even-keeled, and it made my skin break out. I spent a year on these meds with a new temperament and oily skin. It felt freaky, like I was some kind of well-adjusted teenager. I stopped taking it because I'm vain and I'd rather suffer quietly in my head than break out on my forehead. These days I just deal with my ADHD by allowing myself to stare at walls, pace, lose my keys, and find myself with hours and hours of time that I can't account for.

People often seem to think that this "spare time" of mine ought to be filled with trips to the pediatrician, Mommy and Me movies, and annual pumpkin patches. They ask me whether I worry about feeling "unfulfilled" without raising children. When you grow up having a panic disorder, anxiety, and depression since age nine, it's pretty easy to be fulfilled at age thirty-eight just by the knowledge that you're no longer an overmedicated or stressed-out little neurotic. In fact, I'm not only having a second childhood, I feel like I'm finally having a first. The last thing I want to do is bring a kid into all of this fun, leaving me to become the chaperone.

I spent about thirty years of my life being too afraid to travel and constantly worried that I was going to die in a plane crash (*What if this plane crashes?* or sometimes the odd *What if this plane above me falls out of the sky and onto my head?*). I'd like another thirty years of enjoying how I'm totally *not* afraid anymore, and the only child I have time for is my inner one. (She can't believe she's been to Disney World ten times and never had the guts to ride Space Mountain.)

When I was growing up in the 1980s, adults used to let Practical Steps in Preventing Children from Dying slide a little bit—like not mandating seat belts on school buses. Yet they worried incessantly about nuclear war—a thing that might happen but, unless they were Ronald Reagan or Gorbachev, they had absolutely no control over.

I'd always had a general sense of well-being and hope for the future until one fateful weeknight in November 1983 when I suddenly didn't. That was the night that I sat down with my parents at the age of nine and watched the made-for-TV movie *The Day After*. The film portrays a fictional war between NATO forces and the Warsaw Pact that rapidly escalates into a full-scale nuclear exchange between the United States and the Soviet Union.

Apparently Ronald Reagan wrote in his diary that the film was "very effective and left me greatly depressed," and that it changed his mind on the prevailing policy on a "nuclear war." (Thank you, Wikipedia!)

After I watched the movie, I wrote in my diary as well. My sentiment was slightly different from President Reagan's. I wrote, "I hope

I kiss a boy and fall in love before the world ends and that he's the one I die with in the nuclear war." I was such a little romantic.

My elementary school teacher, Mrs. Williams, had very strong feelings about her students watching *The Day After*. She sent all of us fourth graders home with a note, strongly urging our parents to forbid us from watching. When I brought the warning letter home my parents were offended that my teacher had the audacity to tell them how to shield their daughter effectively from a life of post-traumatic stress disorder. I had signed my name on the dotted line, under the promise "I will not watch this movie." My mom put the letter aside. "Jennifah, where was Mrs. Williams when the boys were throwing snowballs at you after school and calling you a geek? She just told me, 'Boys will be boys,' and now she thinks she can send home notes telling me what to let you watch? Maybe if more kids watched this movie, they wouldn't be such little shits on the playground."

Yes. Maybe if more kids watched a supposedly realistic enactment of a nuclear holocaust, kids would be off playgrounds completely and instead roaming the halls of their local mental institutions or in line at the pharmacy for some nice prescription opiates.

I'll never forget the scene where the nuclear bombs from the Soviet Union hit Lawrence, Kansas—all portrayed with that (Emmy-nominated) stock footage of mushroom clouds. Residents of Lawrence, Kansas, are on the highway. The traffic is bumper to bumper. The entire state is desperate to drive away from the three hundred incoming nuclear missiles from Russia, but no one makes it out alive. The sky zaps and rumbles. Flashes of red and orange appear and then a white mushroom cloud rises on the horizon and, just like they're being X-rayed, the people in their cars go from bodies to bones in an instant. Skeletons suddenly sit behind the wheels of cars.

My dad tried to console me with realism. "Jen, this movie isn't completely true. If the Russians bomb us, they'll hit Washington, DC first. Besides, the Russians don't want to nuke us because then we'll nuke *them* off the face of the planet."

The Day After ended with Jason Robards's character nearly

disintegrating into the arms of another man as they sat helpless among the ruins of Lawrence, Kansas. They held each other as they waited for their last breaths. I rabidly read the credits, which assured me that this was just a fictional event. My mother talked over the disclaimers. "You know what I'm realizing? We don't have the right kind of basement for a nuclear war. It's too porous and Ronnie, when are you going to fix that old, rotten cellar door? That's not going to keep out radiation. I guess we could drive to Jennifah's school and stay in the bomb shelter there."

That was news to me. There was a bomb shelter under my school? I decided that I no longer trusted adults. First you have your crazy adults, like the ones who want to run countries and start wars. Then you have your lying adults, like my teacher who pretends war isn't possible even though she's teaching us state capitals directly over a bomb shelter. If there was no way that a nuclear war could happen, why was I forbidden to watch a movie about it? Why didn't my teacher send home a note warning parents not to take their kids to see *Poltergeist*? I now believed that war was imminent and this was everyone's way of educating us about what to do because no one had the guts to just tell us, "We do frequent tests of the Emergency Broadcast System because we know that soon there will be an actual emergency."

The next day on the walk to school I told my best friend, Shannon, about the movie. She hadn't watched it. She declared that her mom grew up in England and knew a lot about Europe and other countries. "So, if there was going to be a war, she would have told me." I felt bad for Shannon. Her naive apocalypse mentality was going to leave her caught by surprise.

FOR A LONG time, I had the coping mechanism to push the utter terror that was known simply as "being alive" to the back of the cupboard of my brain. I loved life. I was a spunky kid. All I wanted to do was to have fun. So despite my grave misgivings about nuclear holocaust, I was still excited for our school field trip to Plymouth Plantation, which is a Disney World–esque pastiche of a rural 1600s community in Plymouth, Massachusetts—home of the Mayflower landing. It's also a place for Boston-area actors to get some work, either a pit stop on their way to their real ambitions or the final resting place of a career that never blossomed. Plymouth Players acted as carpenters, milkmaids, and blacksmiths, carrying on as if it were really the 1600s, demonstrating their skills without any modern conveniences.

Once we were let loose on the plantation, my fourth-grade class immediately began its mission: get one of these pilgrims to screw up and act as if it's 1983, not 1683. I watched the class bully, Greg, mess with a busy Pilgrim woman. "So, do you have milk?" he asked. She answered, "Yes. We get milk from the cow's udders every morning." He said, "Do you put it in the fridge?" She said, "I don't know what that is." He asked her, "Do you have a VCR?" The class burst into giggles and Mrs. Williams warned, "Okay, that's enough." This pilgrim was unfazed. She answered, "Do I have a what? I don't know what that is. But I do have this device, a loom!"

I wandered from the group and over to the edges of the plantation, where the bridge to the present day led right into the gift shop. I recognized a familiar sign discreetly hanging on the wall behind the door, a yellow sign with three triangles meeting in the center. FALLOUT SHELTER. Wait, was Plymouth Plantation a target for a nuclear bomb? Does everywhere have a fallout shelter? One minute I could be browsing the collection of Plymouth Rock refrigerator magnets and Mayflower coloring books, and the next minute I could be underground, taking shelter from a nuclear winter.

Suddenly my thoughts were tumbling over one another like socks in a dryer. *If there is a nuclear war right now, we are going to die on this plantation. If I try to run off this plantation, I'm going to get lost and no one will be able to find me. I can't breathe. What if something is wrong with my lungs?* Even though I was only just standing there, thinking scary thoughts, my body was reacting like I was in the front seat of a roller-coaster carriage, about to careen down the tracks on the first drop.

I got a surge of adrenaline and turned to run back to the plantation, back to 1683, a simpler time when wars were fought with bows and arrows. Then I heard a noise. A plane was flying low overhead and the rumbling shook me. What if it was a warplane carrying a bomb? Suddenly, I couldn't feel my heart beating. Were there secret modern hospitals at Plymouth Plantation or just fallout shelters? I felt alone and on the verge of death while everyone around me kept up this stupid butter-churning charade.

Even with my cardiac arrest, I managed to run back to my group and saw my classmates innocently learning how to shoe a horse. I asked Mrs. Williams, "Why is that plane flying so low? What's going on?" The blacksmith continued banging metal together and denied the very existence of the plane. "What's going on is that I'm preparing a new shoe for our trusty horse." I couldn't stand it. I couldn't have my life risked in order to carry on this facade that it wasn't 1983 and that our lives weren't all in nuclear-level danger. I was possessed by a newfound fearlessness and disregard for authority. I screamed, "Drop the goddamn pilgrim act! It's Armageddon!"

And it happened. I got a pilgrim to drop the act. He wiped his brow with his handkerchief and said to my teacher, "Is she okay?" I felt like I had just come up for air after drowning. The pain in my heart stopped. The rush of speaking up was exhilarating and my knees began to buckle.

Mrs. Williams led me away from the group and the blacksmith continued to heat his coals. My teacher demanded an explanation. I told her that I saw the fallout shelter sign and then the low-flying plane and I wasn't sure whether the air-raid signals like the ones in *The Day After* were working at Plymouth Plantation. Mrs. Williams said, "You watched that movie? Jennifer, nobody else in class watched that movie. I sent home that note." Instead of yelling at me, she took my hand and led me to the parking lot. She told me to relax and sit the field trip out. Mrs. Williams whispered with the bus driver and I spent the rest of the field trip napping on the front seat of a parked bus.

I had no idea that what I'd just suffered was a panic attack—a simple fight-or-flight response that happens to your body and brain when adrenaline takes over. I thought what I experienced were two separate incidents: I was concerned about the fake pilgrims and my real teacher ignoring the fact that nuclear war was imminent, and coincidentally on that very same day, during my confrontation with a fake pilgrim, I happened to have mysterious heart palpitations and chest pains.

Once my mom got wind of this we went straight to the emergency room. I did a stress test—you know, those things that forty-year-old men do on a treadmill with all of those stickers on your chest like E.T. had on in the scene where he was dying. The ER doctor diagnosed me with "stress." That seemed about right to me. I didn't realize I was nine years old. I felt like I was forty. I *was* stressed. I was worried about nuclear war. I was worried about my sister who was getting a divorce and my other sister, who was just starting college but her grades weren't that good. I was worried about my parents, who had been fighting a lot. I had to keep the entire family together! If stress was all that I had—I was pretty damn lucky! I called my sister Violet in her college dorm at UMass Amherst. I told her the good news: "I didn't have a heart attack. I'm just stressed!" She said, "You're nine. You shouldn't have stress. If you're stressed now, you're going to be a nervous wreck when you're a grown-up." She didn't hang up the phone but let it swing back and forth from the pay phone cradle. I heard her run down the hall with her friends, laughing and screaming all the way. Our lives were so different.

I didn't realize until years later at a cocktail party that *The Day After* did not affect everyone of my generation the way it did me. Some people were like, "That movie was so stupid. Did you see that dumb part where everyone turns into a skeleton? My friends and I were laughing." I visited Shannon and her family last Christmas. She bounced her adorable son on her knee and remembered, "Jen, you were always obsessed with the world ending. It was so funny. You used to cut up pictures of Bruce Willis and put them in your shoe because you wanted to be with him when you died. Who thinks about death at age nine, let alone Bruce Willis?"

I was just really glad in that moment that Shannon's kid had her for a mother and not me.

A YEAR BEFORE all of this *Day After* drama, I'd written my last will and testament on a cocktail napkin during a three-hour flight from Boston to Orlando, Florida. I developed a fear of flying the first time I stepped foot on a plane.

My parents and I boarded the now defunct Eastern Airlines plane via an external set of stairs. I felt just like one of the Beatles—except I was not exiting a plane to a hysterical, crying bunch of fans, I was entering a plane with a hysterically crying mother who had just realized how afraid she was to fly. My mom made her way to our seats in coach. My dad put his hand on my shoulder and guided me toward the cockpit. This was, of course, before 9/11/2001. This was just barely after 9/11/1981. You could smoke cigarettes and listen to a Richard Pryor album in the cockpit if you wanted to back in those days. The stewardesses (not yet flight attendants) ushered us into the tiny, low-ceilinged pod. My dad said, "My daughter is apprehensive about flying but I wanted to show her how safe it is!" I hadn't really been apprehensive about flying—but now I was. What if the pilot pressed the wrong button? Would we be ejected from our seats? What if the copilot started goofing around and pulling levers willy-nilly—would the plane take a nosedive? The pilot and copilot shook my hand. They motioned to the gazillion million controls, gadgets, lights, and levers before them. "This is where the magic happens!" the pilot said. My hands got clammy instantly at even the casual thought that the only thing keeping me in the sky would be "magic."

We left the pilots to their gadgetry and magic making. There was one more stop on the airplane tour. My father led me up a mini–spiral staircase to the lounge. I know what you're thinking. What lounge? You mean the metal snack tray that the flight attendant wheels around? No. That's a cart. I'm talking about a lounge; an actual lounge with a bar and alcohol and bar stools. Men and women who looked like they were graduates of Studio 54 sipped drinks, from real glasses, at the bar. Both sexes wore feathered hair and shoulder pads. I thought to myself, *I want my life to be just like this: glamorous, high rolling, and permanently tanned.* Gone were my clammy hands and the memory of the intimidating cockpit. This glamorous world seemed safe. The people at the top of the spiral staircase had no worries. They were jet-setters. Maybe one of these rich people would adopt me and we wouldn't have to tour cockpits or fly coach. I could sit next to my glamorous mom and dad and sip a Shirley Temple while they got bombed on gin. We would travel the world together—always maintaining the perfect amount of fantasy to counteract life's reality.

Soon I went back to coach to join my real mother, who had her rosary beads in her lap. The beads only came out on big occasions— like funerals. When the beads came out it signaled that my mom was in dire need of strengthening her long-distance connection to God. She had taught me once how to pray with rosary beads but I could never remember the routine. I had no interest. Madonna hadn't come out with "Like a Virgin" yet. It would be a little while before I found out how cool they look as an accessory.

I excitedly relayed to my mom that there was a whole other universe/cocktail lounge right above our heads. She snapped nervously at my father, as if he had been the architect of the plane: "Ronnie, there's a bar on this plane? How on earth can this plane hold that much weight? We're not going to make it!"

During takeoff my dad remained silent, fully focused and staring straight ahead, like he was trying not to get seasick on a boat. He gripped our shared armrest. He gritted his teeth and said over and over in a forced singsong, "Here we go! Here we go!" As the wheels left the ground, I realized that I was in the hands of two parents who were anything but grounded themselves. My dad was terrified of flying and the tour of the cockpit had been more to calm his white knuckles than mine. My dad clenched and my mom prayed. I was sandwiched in a chorus of "Here we go!" and "Hail Mary, full of grace . . ."

In that moment, I knew I was going to inherit this rosary-saying woman's fear and this cockpit-touring man's denial. It couldn't be stopped. And the exotic people wearing blue eyeliner upstairs represented a fantasy world, an alternate universe in which I felt I should be living but that I knew was impossible. Later in life, my various therapists have called this sort of thing "conditioning." My mom calls it "We weren't that bad. You have such an imagination."

From then on I could panic on airplanes even if the view was fantastic, even if there was no turbulence, even if the flight attendants were actually smiling that day, even if the pilot said, "This is God. I will be your pilot today and I swear to myself—we will not crash." I could panic even sitting in first class, where they serve warm cookies and champagne. Distractions and logic do not help temper what my psychiatrist explains to me is just some overintense fight-or-flight response that is left over from my caveman DNA. I have nowhere to put my adrenaline on flights, since my inner caveperson cannot club the wild beast that is chasing her and drag it back triumphantly to the cave. There is not enough legroom for that.

After ten years of school-vacation trips to Disney World, at age sixteen I finally called it quits. And it wasn't because I was too cool. I loved Disney World. By the time I was fourteen, I had started to wear all black to the Magic Kingdom and I posed with Mickey wearing a mean scowl, but I secretly wanted to be there while looking like I didn't. I had to surrender my annual trip to the most magical place on earth—or anywhere else that required flight—because my anxiety on airplanes had grown too severe. I couldn't look forward to seeing a palm tree if it meant I had to survive a few hours of sheer terror to get to it.

Not flying for a while didn't cramp my high school life at all. I was happy just staying on the ground and being a teenager in the suburbs of Massachusetts. I went to college in Boston. No planes needed. My goal was to become a famous world-traveling actress who lived on the West Coast. I figured I'd eventually just grow out of my fear of flying in the same way that I had grown out of thinking it looked really defiant to wear floral dresses with black knee-high combat boots.

I sat out spending a semester abroad in Amsterdam during my junior year of college simply because I was too afraid to cross the pond at thirty thousand feet. I watched classmates and friends pack up their backpacks. I stood with them as they convened in the dormitory lobby, waiting for the shuttle that would whisk them to the airport. They would board a plane without worrying about meeting an untimely death. And they would spend three months in Amsterdam living in a converted castle and studying things like Shakespearean Breath Control for Actors. I stayed behind with other nonadventurous people and we suffered through another New England winter, during which my greenskeeper dad would drive his sitting snowplow throughout the golf course and yell at the kids sledding, "Hey, there's grass under there and you're ruining it!"

In retrospect, I'm okay with my decision to remain in Boston while some of my friends lived in the Netherlands. I'm glad I didn't turn into my friend Shane. Shane and I had coffee upon his return and he lit up a marijuana cigarette in the middle of our local café. I grabbed his arm. "Are you crazy?" Shane looked at me, puzzled. "Dude, what?" I grabbed his joint and put it out. "Ohhhh. Yeah. It's against the law. I forgot. Man, I'm just so used to being in a more culturally mature place like Amsterdam where pot is legal."

When I was twenty and living with my parents for the summer before my senior year of college, I decided that I couldn't be afraid to go anywhere anymore. In case I *didn't* naturally outgrow my fear, I didn't want to be stuck in Boston for the rest of my life. So I joined a support group at Boston's Logan Airport in the Delta Airlines terminal. The group was called—and I'm not joking—Logan's Heroes. My fearless leader was Dr. Al Forgione, a clinical psychologist who in twelve weeks was going to rewire our brains so that we associated thoughts of flying with relaxation rather than catastrophe.

Dr. Al handed me a small cup of orange juice and told me to take a seat anywhere at the conference table. At my chair I found a book and a collection of cassette tapes called *Relaxation Exercises for Air Travel*. Dr. Al said, "Flip through the book if you want, but don't look at the pictures on page sixty-eight. You won't be ready for that until week six." I immediately disobeyed the doctor's orders and turned to page 68, where I came face-to-face with a photo of a plane's cockpit. My heart went from zero to high blood pressure and I felt the classic prelude to a panic attack. I couldn't even look at a *picture* of a plane? Shit. I didn't know I had it that bad.

At one point Dr. Al said to me, "What are you doing here? You're too young to have any fears! These years are the best years of your life!"

In my opinion, sitting in an airport with a bunch of terrified middle-age people on a balmy night the summer before one's senior year in college was not anyone's idea of "the best years of your life." I had never considered that I was too young to have fears. I knew that being too afraid to travel abroad put me in the minority at college. But I had expected to come to Logan's Heroes and meet all the other twenty-year-olds who weren't spending a semester abroad finding themselves.

"Get mad at the fear!" This was Dr. Al's motto. Take the rush of adrenaline that fear produces and turn it outward. Screw that fear! How dare that fear creep into our heads and start messing with us. We were in control! The fear was an unwelcome pest. It all sounded empowering in the moment and especially sitting in the safety of a conference room chock full of gravity.

Being a Logan's Hero was hard work. Every week I had to read a page of the *Fearless Flying* book. Every night I was to sit and do a guided meditation. This was called "practicing the relaxation response." Dr. Al was the narrator on the tape. He suggested getting in a comfortable chair and picturing yourself alone on a beach in a quiet, remote location. That's the first time that I realized I also had a fear of being on a beach in a remote location. Was there a hospital in this beach town? How alone was I? What did I eat? Was there shelter in case of a hurricane? I decided that it was best for me to picture myself on a crowded beach, complete with all of the necessary accommodations.

All of us Logan's Heroes took a graduation flight from Boston to New York City and back. Every other Logan's Hero was heroic. They did not panic and used only breathing techniques, no drugs or alcohol, to combat their anxiety on the flight. I didn't use drugs or alcohol either but I couldn't breathe. I white-knuckled the flight and sat next to Dr. Al, making whimpering sounds. When the plane landed, he took me aside and said, "I think there is more going on with you than just a fear of flying. You might want to look into seeing a psychiatrist who can help you with your anxiety. And just remember, this is the time of your life."

Dr. Al was right. I did need a psychiatrist. I finally started seeing one a few years later once the mere fear of having a panic attack caused actual panic attacks in malls, on highways—even while lying quietly in "corpse pose" in yoga class. All that silence and stillness and my brain would start to go crazy: *Hey, Jen, while you have five minutes at the end of class, I thought I'd remind you that you're just a small person stuck on a ball that is spinning through the atmosphere.*

My psychiatrist offered me something that Dr. Al never did. Just like Dr. Al had his motto: "Get mad at the fear!" I now have my own motto: "Have Klonopin, will travel."

It took a lot of therapy and a lot of different antidepressants to rewire my brain. I'm still in therapy but am not medicated—unless you count Skittles. I take Klonopin as needed when I fly and I carry some in my purse just in case. (Please, muggers, if you see me on the street, don't hit me over the head and steal my purse. Psychiatrists never believe you when you say your prescription was stolen.)

I finally understand that it's okay to be a little afraid of things but that obsessing over them does not mean you have any more control over what you fear. There's a big difference between thinking, *Hey, it would suck to die in a nuclear war or a plane crash*, and, *Good morning— oh my God. What if a nuclear bomb hits my home now? Okay, what about now? Now?*

When I turned thirty-five, I finally shook off most of the "fear of life" that had gripped me since before MTV was even a thing. *The Day After*, my parents, and Eastern Airlines are not to blame for the neuroses of my youth. Clearly, other children watched that movie but were comforted by Sting's end credits song, "Russians."

I just happened to be wired to develop panic disorder, depression, and anxiety. Youth was wasted on the young in my case—but I am not going to waste my middle age. In the past two years I've been lucky enough to have my work take me to London, Australia, and almost every state in America. It's afforded me vacations in Paris, Mexico, and Hawaii. There are so many more places I want to see. I've relinquished my responsibilities as the world's sole nuclear war worrywart, and the only child I want to indulge right now is my inner one.

A LOT OF my friends who have kids say to me, "We'd love to travel more and go out every night, but we have a child now. We got that out of our system in our twenties, so now it's just time to settle down." Well, I got nothing out of my system in my twenties and I'm excited about starting to put things in my system. I'm lucky that my friend Sarah doesn't want kids either, and if she ever changes her mind, I'm going to push her down a flight of stairs.

Sarah and I decided to take a trip to Maui together to ring in the 2012 New Year. We figured after we spent Christmas with our respective families, we'd then detox in Hawaii by cooking our skin in the sun and getting salty seawater in our eyes. We both write for *Chelsea Lately* as well as work on other projects, and we travel a lot to do

stand-up. We wanted a vacation where we could do absolutely nothing. (For parents who are reading this, "nothing" is that thing you
will get to do once your kids leave for college, if they ever leave for
college. I hear tuition is skyrocketing.)

We opted to stay at the Grand Wailea Maui. It's a family-friendly
resort. We're not opposed to families existing—we're very generous
that way. Sarah and I were confident that we'd be undisturbed by
screaming toddlers in the cabana we rented at the adults-only pool.

See? There was even a sign at the entrance of the adult pool that
clearly states as much. I don't know anyone who dutifully and without question obeyed authority more than my parents and I when I
was a child. That sign would have put the fear of God in us. If eight-
year-old Jen had even walked *near* this sign on a family vacation, my

mother would have grabbed my arm and harshly whispered, "Jenni-fah, don't go near there, it's for rich people who will have their own private security. They'll have us arrested and we'll have to spend the rest of the vacation in the town jail run by the local mafia."

Seems like kids these days (and their parents) aren't scared of some words engraved on a placard. On our first day in Maui, there was not one adult in the adult pool because there were so many kids swimming (aka peeing) in the four-foot-deep waters. There were tween boys in the hot tub! Just in case you think I'm not being fair, just in case you're thinking to yourself, *Jen, let the children enjoy a refreshing chlorine dip in the hot Maui sun! They're on vacation and they're just kids. This is the time of their lives!* I'll show you Exhibit A (and the only exhibit that I have to offer): On the next page is a map of the pools at the Grand Wailea hotel in Maui:

The only pool for people eighteen and over is the Hibiscus Pool. Children have access to a lazy river, rapids, a water slide, a scuba pool, Pool no. 1, Pool no. 2, Pool no. 3, and even a pool with a swim-up bar for their twenty-one-and-over parents! There was no swim-up bar at the Hibiscus Pool. There was no bar at all. Just a few harried waitresses trying to deliver watered-down drinks while rogue toddlers tripped them up.

My legs were sore from being cramped on a long flight and be-cause I'm thirty-eight now and beginning to feel the fact that I'm slowly rotting from the inside. I wanted to sit in the hot tub but I couldn't because I was self-conscious about sitting in a hot tub with a bunch of twelve-year-old boys who would see me in my bikini. If I wanted to spend my vacation feeling uncomfortable in a bathing suit around boys, I'd buy a round-trip ticket on a time machine and go back to 1987, when I was called "boobless" by two boys back on Duxbury Beach in Massachusetts. Sure, I have boobs now, but I also have a stomach. There was probably a six-month window of time when I was nineteen when my boobs were of a good size and I had no stomach flab—that girl would look great in a bikini if she weren't busy trying to be "grunge" in her oversize flannel shirts.

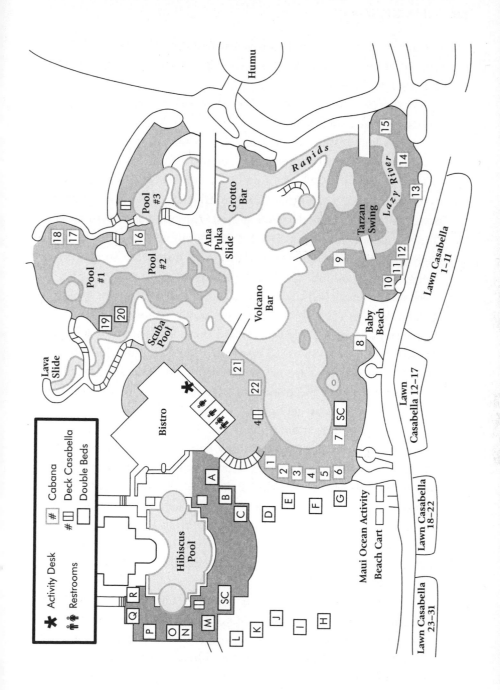

Sarah squinted and looked toward the far end of the pool. She pointed at what appeared to be two eight-year-old girls splashing. "Look! Over there!"

"Where. Is. Their. Mo-therrr?" I asked Sarah, overemphasizing every word like a total bitch.

"I don't know. This is ridiculous," Sarah said. "I mean, there are ten kids' pools here! They need this one too?!"

The waitress arrived and brought us our drinks. "Is everything okay?" she asked. Sarah immediately masked her rage. "Everything's great. Yeah." *Liar.* I nodded and smiled. The waitress walked away. Our confidence came back. "Well, this is total bullshit," I said. "I'm totally going to say something to somebody." Just as the "somebody" I could say "something" to was completely out of reach.

Sarah and I watched the mothers of the children who so boldly ignored *the sign.* The moms sat in their lounge chairs, slathering on their lotion. Mom no. 1 yelled toward the pool in that loud voice that moms are forced to use to be heard above screaming kids.

"Hey, Jessica, come here. Let me put some more sunblock on you! Yes. Yes, you *do* need more sunblock. It's high noon. Jessica! Come here right now. You can get right back in!"

Why didn't Jessica's mom walk over to the pool and talk, in a normal voice, to her child, who shouldn't even have been in the adult pool to begin with? How would I know? I've never had a kid. I don't understand why it's fun to spend a vacation screaming into the ears of your innocent children on a warm Maui afternoon—especially when you end up screaming into the ear of an innocent childfree woman who is just trying to pretend to read her *InStyle* magazine's greatest haircuts edition as she secretly eavesdrops on other cabana conversations.

Then Mom no. 2 yelled to her daughter, who was even farther away than little Jessica. "Ashley, do you want me to get you one of those rubber tubes? Which one do you want? Huh?! Which one?! No, *which one?* The inner tube that you sit in and not the foam roller? Okay. Okay."

Ashley's mom walked past Sarah and me *on her way to the kids' pool to rent a toy for her kid, to bring back for her to play with in the forbidden adult pool.*

As she passed us, I said loudly, "It's not very quiet here today. These cabanas were expensive. It would be nice to have some quiet."

In her best loud-on-purpose voice, Sarah said, "I know. This is the adult pool, right? Kids aren't allowed?"

That was the extent of our confrontation with Ashley's mom—a hopefully-she-heard-us level of passive-aggressive commentary. She returned with an inner tube and Jessica and Ashley climbed in, got comfortable, and floated around in the adult pool, which continued to be populated with nonadults. I felt like I was at a strip club with my family—these things just don't go together.

After a lunchtime margarita, we got a little more confident. Before she could walk away, Sarah said to our waitress, "Um, so, kids aren't allowed in this pool, right? This is the adult pool?"

The waitress agreed. "Yes. This is the adult pool."

Sarah, in her best yeah-I-know-I'm-being-a-C-word voice, asked, "Sooooo, what's that?" pointing at our new nemeses Jessica and Ashley.

The waitress turned and noticed the girls. "Oh," she said. "I don't know."

I added, "And I think those boys in the hot tub are definitely under eighteen." I immediately felt bad for tattling on anyone so I made a joke. "I mean, I'm so bad with guessing ages. They could be thirty for all I know and just really skinny."

The waitress smiled and said, "Well, yeah. This is the adult pool." And with that she turned on her heel to leave.

I summoned all of my courage. "Oh, ma'am? Um, can you come back for a second? Um, is there someone we can talk to about this? I mean, they're not doing anything wrong, but it is the adult pool and we don't care if they're here in general but there is a sign that says no one under eighteen can be here. I mean, it's not my rule. It's yours."

The waitress said, "I'll get a manager."

As she walked away, Sarah high-fived me. "Best passive-aggressive comment of all time. 'It's not my rule. It's yours.' Yes!"

I started to get excited because I noticed a young couple sitting on the edge of the pool, listening to our conversation. I assumed that they also wanted to go into the pool but couldn't because of Ashley, Jessica, and the rest of the Inner Tube Gang. I made eye contact with them as I said to Sarah, "I mean, at least the manager is on the way, because we have to say *something*. These kids shouldn't be in the adult pool!" I think I expected the young couple to stand up and applaud like congresspeople approving my presidential declaration about the state of the adult pool. They looked away from me and started whispering and giggling in each other's ears. I wanted to yell at them, "Oh, fine. Make fun of me. But I'm fighting for all of our rights! Even if you honeymooners change your mind and have kids later in life—right now this is our time by the Hibiscus Pool!"

A manager who looked like he was too young to be allowed in the adult pool himself approached us. He said, "What's going on? Are the kids bothering you guys?"

"Well, no . . . ," Sarah said. "Not exactly."

"They're really well behaved," I said, trying to sound very maternal. "But it's just that this is the adult pool and technically they shouldn't be here. We paid extra money for these cabanas in the quiet area and it's not very quiet."

A toddler ran by with her wet feet slapping against the concrete. One slip and her head would split open like a dropped coconut. I gripped my lounge chair, feeling helpless, and blurted out, "Oh my God. Be careful. Be careful, honey." I turned to the teenage manager. "See?" I pleaded. "I can't handle this."

He said, "Okay. I'll talk to someone about it," and scurried away, passing the hot tub full of leering boys without saying a word.

Our cabana quickly became Child Watch Headquarters. Sarah and I grabbed our laptops and took advantage of the free WiFi connection. We got to work. I took to Twitter and started tweeting to the Grand Wailea hotel, asking them, "What's your policy on kids who crash the adult pool? We have a situation here." Sarah got the general manager's information off the Grand Wailea website. She picked up her BlackBerry, made a call, and left a very stern message with the general manager's assistant.

"What did she say?" I asked.

"She said that he'd call me back later today. She wouldn't take down my cell phone number. She said he could just call me back in the room."

The general manager would return a customer's complaint call to her room? Who sits in her room in the middle of the day when she's on vacation in sunny Maui? You know who *should* be sitting in their room in the middle of the day—parents and their toddlers. Those kids need a nap.

I'd had enough bullshit. I was going to take a bullet for my partner in Child Watch crime. "You wait here, Sarah. I'm going in and there's no need for you to see this." I put on my sandals and angrily flip-flopped off toward the check-in desk to confront the person who had handed me two plush towels that morning.

The towel girl was suspiciously nice and she said that she'd call security for me. Okay. Now we were getting somewhere. *Security.* I went back to the cabana and Sarah and I watched and waited for security. I was ready for plastic handcuffs to be slapped on some toddlers and their rule-breaking moms. While we were waiting we spotted a heavy preteen girl whose boobs had not grown as round as her thighs and stomach just yet. She seemed awkward and unhappy. She held her tired-looking mom's hand as they walked around the adults-only pool, looking for lounge chairs. Sarah and I shared a look.

"She can stay," I said.

"Yeah," Sarah agreed. "She'd probably get bullied by some assholes at the kids' pool. Who knows what she may have already been through."

"Yeah," I said, "she's obviously got some weird enmeshment shit going on with her mom too. They can't be apart and this girl seems like an old soul."

Just then a towering, broad-shouldered black man in uniform rounded the corner. Here he was. *Security.* Tiny heads are gonna roll. Then the towering, broad-shouldered black man in uniform walked right by the boys in the hot tub, strolled past the preteen girls in the pool, and darted around the toddlers running on the pool's edge. We watched him walk off into the bright sun back toward the hotel. Sarah was speechless, so I can't really capture her reaction in print. It was a series of guttural sounds and wild hand gestures, like someone trying to make a *w* sound for the first time. "Don't worry, partner," I told her. "I'm going back out there."

I got up and ran after the security guard, this time barefoot, hopping and saying, "Ouch, hot, ouch," with every step. "Hey, security guy. What *was* that out there? You're just going to walk by?" He said, "I think they got the message." "What message? That security means nothing? That if they keep wading in the adult pool, security might . . . walk by again? Ooooh, scary. You have to actually *say* something to the kids, like, 'Hi, you kids don't look like you're old enough to be here. You must leave this pool if you don't get your period yet or have never had a wet dream.'"

He followed me back to the adult pool and talked to the kids and their parents. I went back to Child Watch Headquarters and let Sarah know that it had all been taken care of. "Uh, then what's that?" Sarah asked. I looked and just as *Security* was walking away, the kids were getting back into the pool. Sarah and I retired from our beat that afternoon and ordered four more margaritas—well, we ordered six, but the waitress gave us a dirty look and said, "My tray only holds four." And in a not-so-subtle way she said, "Four is a good limit. Dontcha think, girls?"

I SAT DEFEATED in Child Watch Headquarters, watching the kids finally get out of the pool as the sun started to go behind the clouds. I hadn't yelled. I hadn't said anything mean to the kids or about the kids to their parents. But I felt like a monster. How come I felt so guilty about wanting the rules to be enforced so that I could enjoy our vacation the way I paid for it?

It was the hotel's rule that there was a separate pool for adults. Why can't the two pools coexist without the generations crossing? It wouldn't dawn on me to go act like an adult in the kids' pool. I wouldn't jump in the shallow end with a drink in my hand and start talking loudly to Sarah in front of a toddler about the best way to prevent a urinary tract infection after sex.

It's so taboo to say that you don't really enjoy the company of children. May I point out that the adults who brought their kids to the adult pool obviously did so because *they* did not want to be around only other children? Do they get a free pass because they procreated? I see parents all the time who get a kick out of saying, "I only like *my* kids. I don't like other kids." But if a single woman without children says, "I don't like kids," she sounds like a sociopath. I realize that one of those boys in the hot tub or girls in the pool could be president someday. I realize that we have children's futures in our hands and they have our futures in theirs. I acknowledge that it's a beautiful cycle and I'll admit that I made myself tear up just typing that sentiment. I don't want to be made to feel like a bitch because I'm upset that now, before those kids grow up to be president, they are peeing in my pool.

Sarah and I went back to our room and enjoyed some champagne on our balcony while we watched the sun set. We also maybe threw a pillow or two off the ledge. We also maybe threw an entire bag of Skittles, one by one, off the balcony at the people walking below (no, no children were harmed). We were well aware that throwing things off a balcony was against the rules, but we knew that the security and management team would be too lazy to bust us unless we told on ourselves.

I GOT HOME from the vacation to find out that there was a new upstairs neighbor in my fourplex apartment building—three new neighbors actually: a mommy, a daddy, and a toddler. My landlord made the executive decision to let a toddler live above a quiet, single woman who works from home as a writer on weekends. I long for the days when the twenty-six-year-old drunk girl lived upstairs and faked really loud, operatic orgasms until four in the morning. At least with her, I could count on the fact that she'd pass out immediately after and she'd stay asleep until about one o'clock the next day. (And if I was in the right mood, let's be honest, it was scintillating to listen to the noises she was making.)

I'm sitting in my home office, typing, and I can hear him now, running up and down the length of his apartment. He sounds like he has weights in his shoes. Every once in a while he stops running, only to drop and then drop again a toy that sounds like a regulation-size bowling ball. I can hear his dad chasing him down the hallway playfully, which makes little Tony (I named him Tony) squeal with delight. Can we all admit that the sound of a kid squealing, even if it's with joy, sounds like squealing? I can angrily press the button on an air horn or I can press the button on an air horn with a sense of carefree fun and either way it sounds like an air horn.

I woke up at five in the morning today because that's what time Tony wakes up—or at least it's the time that he starts crying and screaming and then choking on the phlegm he's built up from crying, and then screaming because he thinks he's going to die from choking on phlegm. Luckily, my dad taught me ingenuity. I put a fan on the floor. I turn it on low and it makes just enough of a sound to create some white noise. If I close my bedroom door, I can't hear a thing that's going on outside of my bedroom—which includes any smoke alarms in the hallway, my home security alarm, or a murderer if he decides to break a window in my kitchen so he can climb through and grab those enticing knives on my counter because he forgot to bring his own weapon. If only these parents upstairs knew just how selfless I was—putting aside my own peace of mind for a little peace and quiet because I know that there's no way I can march upstairs and tell a toddler to stop crying about how he doesn't understand yet that sleeping is fucking awesome.

I took to my Facebook page to get some advice about this situation with Toddler Tony. I asked my friends who were parents to tell me whether there is ever a good time or a good way to talk to the parents upstairs. Was it out of line for me to ask Tony's parents to not let him run while wearing shoes? It's a lot nicer than what I really wanted to ask, which was, "Why don't you take Tony outside, you fucking morons? It's a permanent seventy-five degrees in Los Angeles and you have this kid cooped up inside an apartment for eight hours straight?"

My friends' comments ran the gamut from unhelpful to infuriating. Suggestions like: "Bake some cookies and bring them up to the new neighbors and slip into the conversation, ever so subtly, that you know of a good park in the neighborhood. Maybe they will get the hint that they should take Tony outside more and it could help educate them about the neighborhood." They lost me at "bake cookies." Bake? Cookies?

I made sure to phrase my Facebook question in a very pro-kid light. I was even gracious enough to admit that one can't expect a kid to ever be completely quiet. Of course, some casual acquaintances of mine who have kids responded:

Jen, sometimes you just have to let a kid be a kid. As a parent, I know this from experience. It's a tough, underappreciated job, having kids. May I suggest noise-canceling headphones?

I haven't had time to bake any cookies (or buy any ingredients), and I'm definitely not up for wearing headphones around my house ten to twelve hours a day. But I have found a solution that works for me. Every time I hear Tony running up and down the entire length of the apartment upstairs and squealing, *"Aahhhhhhhhhhhhhh!"*—I put on a pair of high heels and I run up and down my hardwood-floored hallway, stomping and clunking and also yelling, *"Aaaaaaahhhhhhhh!"*

at the top of my lungs. (I don't have any downstairs neighbors—unless you count the termites underneath our complex.)

I'm hoping that Tony's parents get the hint and realize that they are not living in a soundproof building. So far, even if they have gotten the hint, the noise hasn't stopped. But I'm actually having a ball. It's so therapeutic and freeing, I just might cut back my therapy sessions from weekly to biweekly. And if Tony's parents stop by to complain, I'll just ever so subtly inform them that my inner kid needs to be a kid and that I know from experience how hard it is to raise one.

4. Married . . . Without Children

If it was a Tuesday night in 2004, I was hanging out at the M Bar, a supper club that housed a popular night of stand-up comedy in a strip mall on Vine at Fountain in Hollywood. I was on a bit of a comedy hot streak—I mean as much of a hot streak as a stand-up comic can have who is performing unpaid for fifty people who are all crammed in the back of the room, trying to avoid sitting at a table because they're too broke to order the stale bruschetta. My hot streak was because I was single and I'm never funnier than when I'm feeling dejected and undersexed. I'd just come to the natural end of a love relationship with (aka I was dumped by) Thomas, who had decided that it would be an improvement in his life to get back together with Hariette, his adult-Goth ex-girlfriend with a death wish. I should have known. He talked about her incessantly and I couldn't keep anything in the nightstand drawer on the side of his bed that I slept on because it was full of her cards and letters from their fucked-up relationship. One card had dried blood and a rose on the inside. Yes, I read the cards. How else should I have amused myself while he was taking a shower or sleeping? This was before the Instagram app or Netflix Instant was invented.

I joked onstage about the band Weezer one night at M Bar and the guy who acted as the comedy show DJ played one of their songs as I left the stage. I couldn't see him, but I knew that this mysterious figure in the booth had been listening closely to my act. *That's thoughtful*, I thought to myself, and went to the bar for a drink. At the bar the mysterious DJ introduced himself to me. His name was Matt. "Nice to meet you," I said.

"We've met a million times before and every time you say it's nice to meet me," Matt said.

"Oh," I answered. "You're a really good DJ. Where else do you work?"

He smiled and said, "I'm not a DJ for a living. I just play music for this show. We've also had this same exact conversation a few times."

I wish I could say that normally I hate being called on the fact that I'm terrible with names, faces, and conversations that happened more than five minutes ago, and that when Matt called me on it I immediately responded positively and realized that I needed this man in my life to love and guide me and help me stay present and in the moment. Nope. I thought, *Well, that's no fun—being called on my shit.* And then I ended up going home and washing the dishes that my clinically depressed roommate had left in the sink.

SPRING CAME AND went. I found myself still thinking about Thomas and doing drive-bys past his apartment complex. I know that when someone in Los Angeles claims to do a drive-by, that person usually has gold teeth and a hit rap song, but I just mean that I was circling his block to make sure his car was in the driveway so I could come to the auspicious conclusion that Thomas was home, forlorn and missing me.

On our first date Thomas had told me that his most cherished book from childhood was Judy Blume's *Superfudge*. The night that Thomas and I ended our relationship (aka when he dumped me as I cried snots out of my eyes on his bedroom floor and begged him to reconsider), he told me that he wanted to reconnect with his childhood and that he had lost himself.

One evening in May, after not having been Thomas's girlfriend for eight weeks, six days, and four hours, I decided that I'd cement myself as a shoo-in for the Museum of Most Romantic Gestures. I went on a hunt for a hardcover copy of *Superfudge*. At the Barnes & Noble cash register, my eyes welled up as I thought about the very John-Hughes-movie moment I was about to enact. I sat in my car outside of Thomas's house, inscribing the inside front cover with "Dear Thomas, you haven't lost yourself. He was here all along." I took a moment of silence to be moved by my sentiment—and briefly wondered whether he would have preferred it written in my blood.

I walked up to his door and at the last minute realized that just dropping the book off would leave our fate up to chance. I wanted to present the one-of-a-kind *Superfudge* to Thomas in person, watch him read the dedication in front of me, and then collapse into my arms with cries of, "You've changed my life! I was such a fool to let you go. Come inside my apartment and come inside my . . . heart. We'll set fire to the Hallmark Hariette nightstand and build our own future with a nice bedroom ensemble from IKEA. Listen, we can't afford anything better right now, but surprisingly they have many bedroom furniture options that don't look like plywood and thick cardboard that's been Scotch-taped together. I may have a nervous breakdown about my lack of manhood when I'm forced to assemble the nightstands with three beers in my system and a faulty Allen wrench, but we'll get through it!" I knocked. Thomas opened the door, saw me, and slammed the door in my face. I heard him frantically affix the door chain.

He yelled from behind the safety of this barricade, "Give me a minute!" I heard whispering. I heard a hysterical girl accuse, *"Who is that?"* I heard Thomas answer, "Hariette, go into the bedroom. This will only take a second." Thomas unchained the door and opened it. He looked at me and whispered loudly, "What?" I handed him the book. I guess I thought that it was worth a try even though it was probably not the best idea to rekindle a relationship with someone who had another girl over and who had just slammed a door in my face.

He took the book and studied it. I started to explain. "Thomas, you once said this was your favorite book from childhood and—"

"Oh, Jen," he said. He didn't say "Oh, Jen" in a romantic "Take me, Jen!" way, but more like I had just spilled oatmeal on the floor from my high chair. He pitied me and knew that it was pointless to yell because I clearly didn't know better. "It's over, Jen." He handed the book back to me. I became indignant. *If you would just reread* Superfudge, *Thomas, you would know that you and I were meant to be together. I have no idea what the fuck even two words are from* Superfudge, *but I have my heart set on this dramedy I've written in my head and there can be no rewrites.*

Thomas shut the door and I heard him twist both dead bolts. He said, "Hariette? Hariette? Come here, honey." I got up and left *Superfudge* on his doorstep. It was just like when I threw a copy of the Albert Camus book *The Stranger* to Robert Smith onstage when I saw the Cure in high school. I'd read that their song "Killing an Arab" was based on that book and I wrote a wistful fan letter on the inside flap that was more of an argument as to why I was Robert Smith's only living soul mate and how unfortunate it was for him to have gone this long without me in his life. In both instances I never got a response. But at least I'm spreading to many men the joy of reading.

ONE NIGHT SHORTLY after the *Superfudge* debacle, I got offstage after my set at M Bar and headed to the bar. A married male comedian—a friend of mine—stopped me to chat. I didn't think this was anything out of the ordinary; he always loved to talk comedy and give advice. He said that a bunch of people were going next door to a bar for a postshow drink and I should come by.

When I got there it was just him. He started to confess that being married is hard and he wanted to know my opinion as a single woman on this complicated issue. Before I could answer, he asked me whether I thought that his jerking off in front of me would be considered cheating on his wife. I wasn't sure of the answer, in part because he was a dozen pounds overweight and wore a crooked hairpiece that resembled a golf course divot. I wasn't attracted to him. If he were Robert Downey Jr. and RDJ wanted to know whether I thought his jerking off in front of me was cheating, I would have said absolutely not. Not only is it not cheating, I think it's good for America if you show me your cock. And if you are at all tired from touching yourself, please allow me to do it for you.

But just as I was about to say, "Look, you're really funny but I have no interest in seeing your dick," I heard a familiar voice behind me say hello. I turned around and saw Matt. He said jokingly, "I know. You don't remember me. But I'm Matt. We've met. I'm not a DJ."

That was the moment. He called me on my shit. I laughed. And I realized that for the last ten years I'd been wearing a sheet over my head like a shitty Halloween ghost costume and that's why I kept picking the bad candy out of the bunch.

My comedian friend immediately pulled out pictures of his kids from his wallet and acted like, "Oh, hey, everyone. You walked in just in time. I was just telling Jen how great my family is. Here's Johnny on his fifth birthday. Isn't he cute?" I subtly turned my back to concentrate on Matt.

It turns out he was from a small beach town in Massachusetts, and I bonded with him by telling him I was from a suburb near the city. He reminded me that we had already discussed this several times. I was starting to think I either had multiple personalities or was just a complete asshole. Apparently it's hard to pay attention to the guy right in front of you who is ready to create a story with you when you're busy obsessing about what to write to a guy who doesn't like you in a copy of *Superfudge* that he didn't ask for.

Matt and I talked about how excited we were that it was almost August and the Red Sox were still having a good season. I know nothing about baseball. I don't know the stats of each player. I don't even know the last name of each player. I don't know what RBI stands for. I don't understand why with all of those steroids those baseball players are so fat.

But I specifically liked the 2004 Red Sox team. They were a ragtag bunch of millionaires who grew their hair long, as opposed to their bitter rivals, the Yankees, a more obedient group of millionaires, who under the supervision of owner George Steinbrenner were forbidden to wear their hair long or have facial hair below the lip. (In baseball this is called "discipline." But when a woman suggests that her boyfriend cut the hair on his scalp and chin area, that's known as "This controlling chick is telling me what to do.")

In case you didn't know because you've been living in a vacuum-sealed hut off the coast of New Zealand or are a Goth teenager, the Red Sox hadn't won a World Series since 1918 and were known as having an eighty-six-year-old "curse" on their heads. The superstition started after the Sox sold Babe Ruth to the New York Yankees in the off-season of 1919–1920. Before the sale of "the Bambino" the Red Sox had been a successful baseball franchise. The 2004 Red Sox referred to themselves as "the Idiots"—an almost Zen declaration that the game they played was one of camaraderie, hope, and joy. It was to be played one pitch at a time and it didn't matter whether there was a curse or how many RBIs (whatever those are) a guy had.

Most people from Massachusetts know a little bit about the ride of Paul Revere but "a lot a bit" about the curse of the Boston Red Sox. It served as a metaphor for all of our lives on an as-needed basis. If something didn't go right in your life, you could remember that nothing was going right for the Red Sox either. The entire state was cursed. The entire state was an underdog. Sometimes things don't work out and maybe we're working against a punishing power higher than ourselves that doesn't want us to win. That kind of "I'm the piece of shit that the world revolves around" attitude is unique to Massachusetts and I think it's why so many comedians are from Boston, and why most people in Boston are sarcastic, angry, and wicked drunk.

• • •

WHEN I TURNED thirty a few weeks later I was still single and threw myself one of those parties that is no longer appropriate past the age of thirty—the type where you send out an Evite and ask everyone to meet you at a bar and pay for their own drinks. I heard that Matt showed up that night, although I didn't see him. I was busy flirting with an artist who, according to my friend, thought I was cute. I think the only reason he thought I was cute was because we had met months earlier at a party and I completely ignored him. Not on purpose. I just didn't know he was there.

If I like a guy, I *can't* ignore him. I can only try to own and occupy him like a celebrity does a small island. I followed the Artist back to his house in a drunken stupor after my party. I slept over. We made out. I fell asleep halfway through our fooling around so I really did only "sleep" with him. The next morning, the sunlight streaming through his window and onto his bed made me self-conscious. Who knows what kind of cellulite could have developed overnight as I transitioned from age twenty-nine to thirty? I left and hoped that he would call me. He didn't call me. I called him. A lot. A week later, I invited him to see *Manhattan* at a revival theater. (He had told me on my birthday that it was his favorite movie.) He said he couldn't go. But why would he not want to see it with me after he told me it was his favorite movie? It couldn't be because I had called him fifty times since we had first met, right? At least I didn't drop a special-edition DVD of *Manhattan* on his doorstep—only because I couldn't remember where he lived.

September rolled around and I hadn't run into Nice Matt from Boston anywhere. I decided that it was time to invite him to my regular Sunday-night karaoke party. I'd never once actually corralled a group of people together for a Sunday-night karaoke party, but Matt wouldn't know that. Besides, I'd always wanted to be the type of girl who has a regular Sunday-night karaoke gathering. I sent out an e-mail to a bunch of friends—including Matt—and said, "It's a Sunday Night Karaoke Party! At the usual place—Sardo's in Burbank." Interestingly, nobody wrote back to say, "What the hell are you talking about? We don't have a regular karaoke night. Are you trying to get something going with a boy?"

Matt showed up. I sang my usual karaoke song, Janis Joplin's "Piece of My Heart"—if you ever see me sing that song at karaoke, it means I'm trying to impress you. And if you're a cute boy, it means I'm trying to get you to impress your penis on me.

Later Matt sang a nervous rendition of "Brandy (You're a Fine Girl)" by Looking Glass. Eventually we were the last ones there. It was like our friends and the patrons of Sardo's were trying to make the decision for us. Come on, you two, make a move already!

You know when you want to make out with someone and you're pretty sure that he wants to make out with you because you're both touching each other's arms? You think to yourself, *This is Body Language 101. He's touching my arm because he knows it's sending me a signal that he's interested. But wait, who would be so obvious and actually touch someone's arm? He's not reading* Cosmo. *Maybe he touches everyone's arm. I've never hung out with him before. That could be his "thing." I better not act on this and ask him if he wants to leave and go somewhere else. Nope. His flirtation is so by-the-book that I'm suspicious. We should just keep sitting knee to knee in this booth and ignoring the fact that we are blind to everyone else at our table but each other.*

Eventually he walked me to my car because he is a gentleman and because my car was right next to his.

We started talking and talking . . . and talking, because it was easier than one of us making the awkward first move. I offered super-smoothly, "Hey, so, if we're going to keep talking, we might as well sit in my car. It's cold." It wasn't cold. Matt got in the front seat and I immediately pounced on him. He flinched. When we talked about it later he said that it just seemed like I was about to hit him. To be fair, I do have a lot of testosterone and I did come at him like a flying squirrel, but I landed like a butterfly and found myself having my first kiss with the man who would become my husband. (I mean, not that night, although there was a ceremony of sorts when Matt had to pee in between our cars.)

The whole next day I tried to remember what song he had sung at karaoke so I could buy it, but I didn't want to ask him what the song was because I knew that if you asked a guy what song he sang at karaoke, he would know you're planning to buy it and listen to it over and over while reimagining your first kiss. I was thirty, but I was not naive.

Matt and I spent the next week fucking off at our day jobs and e-mailing each other all day instead—those types of stories that you've told a million times and can't wait to have a new audience for. He told me his favorite childhood memory about the time his middle school gym teacher murdered his wife and claimed that the blood on the walls was marinara sauce. I reminisced about the time that a priest at our church wore a lavaliere microphone and ranted in his Sunday sermon about how gay people were destroying parades because they throw condoms off floats and into the street, and he let out a fart under his robe that was amplified through the speakers that hung next to the stations of the cross on the sides of the church.

I don't know why that happens—that when you're hanging out with someone you know you're going to fall in love with, you just don't know where to begin and you start picking up pieces of your life as though they're old photos randomly gathered in a box and handing them over to a virtual stranger for safekeeping. It's like saying, "Here. I'm excited and hopeful and I don't know where to begin but I think one day we'll eventually have enough time to unpack this thing and make some sense of it all."

When the Red Sox won the World Series in October 2004, I felt like I had reversed my curse too. I wanted to tell Matt that I loved him but I didn't want to overwhelm us. (We were already crying like a couple of postmenopausal women who had just won bingo on a seniors cruise.) I liked a boy who liked me back. He wasn't a creep who only wanted a one-night stand. He didn't find me more attractive the more unavailable I was. We were grown-ups.

Except for one thing. He was renting a bedroom in the very nice house owned by his always-home-and-hogging-the-living-room friend. I was sleeping on a borrowed (stolen) futon from a(n) (ex-)friend while renting a small apartment the size of a Cracker Jack box that was across from an actual crack house with my constantly suicidal and oft wailing friend Krista. Without our own places and living in neighborhoods we either couldn't afford on our own or couldn't afford to move out of, Matt and I were not grown-ups. We were grown-up-adjacent.

BECAUSE I'M A stand-up comedian and I talk honestly about my life onstage, and because he was obviously lurking around my gigs all the time, waiting for me to forget I'd met him, Matt knew intimate details about my life before he and I ever had our first conversation. One of the first sentences Matt ever heard me utter was a joke that goes, "When I'm in love with someone it doesn't dawn on me to want to have their baby. I just don't think I've ever had that urge to . . . ruin our lives." So by the time we went on our first date, we'd already had an important (albeit one-sided) discussion about me not wanting to have children.

Matt knew what he was getting into with me—or what he was not getting into, like late-night feedings (except for my two-in-the-morning burrito cravings). After we finally said "I love you" and realized that our thing was going somewhere, because neither of us was looking to go anywhere (else), I revisited the kids topic with Matt almost monthly—and not just when my period was late.

I was very concerned with making certain that Matt was absolutely sure that he didn't want children. I didn't want him to just go along with what I was saying simply because his current circumstances led him to not even be able to fathom what having a kid would be like. I wanted Matt to picture himself coming home at night to a pregnant me, lying on the couch in my elastic-waist jeans, yelling for him to bring me a diet ginger ale and then screaming when he brought it to me because he did it wrong. I wanted it in a glass with *lots of ice.* He had to start thinking like a girl, obsessing over the future and daydreaming about our childfree life together. I know guys don't normally picture anything beyond the next pair of boobs they might be seeing naked.

Matt and I had a State of Our Union a few times a year, not just to talk about how we felt about kids (they should be banned from airplanes and not allowed to touch *every single* elevator button with their germ-laced fingers) but also to talk about what we wanted out of life. We both agreed that what was most important was the freedom to do what we wanted, whenever we wanted, whether that meant pick up and travel, move, change jobs, quit jobs, take four jobs—things that require the freedom of not having a family to provide for. I did *not* want to be one of those women who were willing to travel as long as they had the time to squeeze all of their breast milk into many three-ounce travel-size bottles. Matt sometimes worked on projects that had him sleeping all day and staying up all night, which is not conducive to child rearing unless you are a vampire. And I know vampires are considered sexy by groups of misguided tween girls who are taught to love men who could potentially kill them, but the reality is that vampires make bad dads and shitty husbands. They hibernate all day and then disappear at sunset—never able to tuck their own kids in at night.

For Matt, it was a decision not to be a dad, rather than a non-feeling. He said he didn't make the decision in a day—it was just a shift from ambivalence to "no fucking way" over time. He likes how unscheduled his life can be. In his own words he says, "I can spend time alone if I want. I can make career decisions without restriction." And perhaps the best reason of all: "Kids? What the fuck am I going to do with a kid?"

WE HAD A dream engagement. He proposed to me on a hot summer night in July under a full white moon from our private balcony at a small bed-and-breakfast in Malibu. After I said yes, we went to a restaurant and sat on the romantic beachfront patio right next to another couple and their three screaming children.

I can't blame the kids. It's fun to scream on a semideserted beach on a summer night. I screamed when Matt proposed and I promptly ran into the ocean in my dress. I didn't know that salt water would cause it to disintegrate. The couple with their three screaming children probably wondered why this man was taking this hobo woman in a shredded lace maxidress to dinner and why she couldn't get through any bites of her food without crying and saying, "No. No. These are happy tears. We're engaged!"

I realized that what made it possible for this couple to keep the romance alive was taking their kids to local paradises like Malibu instead of a Chuck E. Cheese's in a strip mall. At least once the kids were asleep, they could listen to the waves crash against the rocks, snuggle, and talk shit while digesting a four-star dinner: "What the fuck is wrong with them? Why do they scream in public? Why do we do this to ourselves?" I imagine going to bed with your husband after your kids have ruined your nice dinner out to be similar to the time that Matt and I bonded over his psycho ex-girlfriend showing up at a party just to yell at him for not liking her anymore.

One year later Matt and I stood at the altar of a nondenominational church, getting married by our Jewish justice of the peace, who was once my elementary school librarian. We wrote our own vows. There were two mentions of Bob Fosse and zero mentions of children. (At her wedding, fifteen years earlier, my sister Violet had acquiesced to having a Catholic mass. When the priest asked the traditional question, "Will you accept children lovingly from God, and bring them up according to the law of Christ and the Church?" she answered, "Yes." She turned to me immediately after and mouthed, "No.")

By the time I got married, a Catholic mass for their daughter was no longer important to my parents. Their biggest concern was that I help pay.

Matt and I went from table to table, thanking our family for attending, which is the most illogical of all wedding reception traditions. We just got married. Can't we fucking sit down and eat? We have to watch our salads wilting at our special little table for two as we visit every relative who is already half in the bag? Our pinot grigio–breathed aunts kissed me on the lips more times during the reception than Matt kissed me. A few of our relatives hadn't heard yet that we didn't plan to have children and made some jokes as we thanked them for coming. There was a lot of, "You two better get to work! You're a little behind!" In other words, "Jen is older than you and pretty soon she won't even get her period anymore." I wished we'd included this in our vows: "Dear Matt, I promise to love you. You're a good egg. Speaking of which, I probably only have one egg left. I'm comforted by this but still paranoid about having some 'miracle' pregnancy. I vow to always take my birth control pill at the same time every night and am hoping that you might continue to use condoms as a backup until I hit menopause."

Some people didn't just ask Matt and me when we were going to have kids but took it a step further with, "Why would you *get* married if you don't want to have kids?"

I had no idea that marriage was only supposed to be between two people who wanted to get between the sheets and make more people. What ever happened to marrying for love—or to get on your partner's health insurance policy, or for presents? No one was going to buy two people in their thirties a four-slice toaster if we just continued to live in sin.

The next question always seemed to be: "But what if your husband changes his mind and starts to resent you?" The way I see it, when you marry someone, you ask him or her to take a vow in front of friends, family, and God, promising to pay your bills if you need it, take care of you when you're sick, and not have sex with anyone else *ever again*. I have a feeling there will be plenty of opportunities for resentment.

When I asked Matt what he said to people who constantly harassed him about when he would procreate and then refused to accept his answer, he told me, "I just say no. That typically ends it."

Matt has a gift for soft-spoken brevity. Whereas I was always inviting him up to my cabin on Riled-Up Mountain—I tend to live at the top of it.

But, Matt, doesn't it bother you that people assume that you have no say in the matter? People look at you as some helpless guy who can't plant his seed because I'm so frigid.

Matt remained calm. "I wouldn't tolerate people looking at me like that."

Then again, how many people were really asking Matt about "our" plans to procreate? His friends were more focused on our plans to make sure that we always had an emergency pack of Camel Lights in our newly acquired hutch (thanks, Crate & Barrel gift registry!) for them to smoke if they got drunk at our place.

Some women tell me that I have to make the decision *for* my husband. They say that whether a man wants kids or not, he doesn't have a biological clock, so he's not paying attention to timing, which is the same reason men can't be trusted to accept a kick under the table from a woman who wants to leave a boring dinner party. I know a woman who says that even though her husband isn't ready to have children, she doesn't want to fight about it and the day she's ready, she's just going to "forget" to take her birth control pill. Listen, if I could take two birth control pills, I would. And I'm glad Matt doesn't have the same hormones I do. Thank God, because one person crying at those Sarah McLachlan commercials about adopting abused one-eyed dogs is enough in one household.

I REMEMBER THERE was one moment when I tried to muster up the desire to have children. Matt and I had just moved in together. I got work on TV about once a year and I was performing on the road at comedy clubs occasionally, but nothing was sticking. I had to admit that against my wishes, I basically had a professional hobby. I did not have a career. I was working as a temp to make ends meet. I was filing contracts for a law office in a windowless room. The only person in the office with a worse job than mine was the pimply intern who had to make ID badges for new hires. He came by my desk with a Polaroid camera to snap my photo (by the way, I think those kinds of photos actually do steal your soul). He said, "I know you. Do you do stand-up? I've seen you around." I shushed him violently, spitting all over his camera, knowing what was about to happen if anyone overheard him. And right on cue the two women I worked for turned around and said, "You're a comedian? You don't seem funny. Tell us a joke!" I wanted to tell them the one about the girl who thought her life was going to be vastly different by the time she turned thirty-two.

I couldn't see the future that I wanted. It seemed so impossible. It was easier to picture the future that I didn't want—me moving back to Needham, Massachusetts, and working in my former high school as the substitute teacher for the tenth-grade drama class and saying things like, "You kids think you understand *Death of a Salesman*? It's not just about not making a sale—it's about disappointing everyone who counts on you but eventually realizing that nobody ever counted on you because you're a ghost of a person." But I had romantic love. And maybe love was all I was going to have. Some people don't even have that, right? I thought maybe it would be nice to get to stay home every day, taking care of a baby instead of temping, and who needed to be out every night doing stand-up at Joan's Pizza Place's Thursday Night Open Mic? If I had a baby, surely my hormones would kick in, I'd become really Zen like the Red Sox, and my life would be devoted to our kid. I could even be a funny mom! Maybe that was the master plan for me all along.

But somewhere deep down I knew that being a mother wasn't right for me. And by "deep down" I mean that when I pictured having a baby instead of pursuing my dreams, I would immediately feel sick; it felt like my intestines were trying to unwind and slither out of my butt.

My ex-boyfriend Thomas would always say, "When are you going to get this comedy thing out of your system? I'm ready to move to

Northern California and start a family." And then by beer number four the dream became "I'm just going to go back to New Hampshire and open up a small revival movie theater. You can come with me. We'll have a family."

Thomas had had a mean father who was also a photographer. Unlike his father, Thomas was actually great at photography. Unfortunately he kept his pictures half developed and hidden in his closet. I wanted to invite people over to look at the work in his closet and tell them it was an art installation called *Hit-You-over-the-Head Symbolism*. He didn't know how to go for his dreams but he was convinced that once a baby was born, that would replace his dream. His life would be solved. He wouldn't have to try and maybe fail and disappoint himself or his father in the process, then somehow he'd make enough money showing screenings of *Casablanca* in a rural town to buy the family some diapers and Campbell's soup and Daddy some Merit Ultra Lights and a six-pack of Budweiser. And then by beer number six Thomas's plan was to move to Mexico and work with animals just like his favorite guy, Jeff Corwin from Animal Planet. Even if I wanted to go to Mexico with him, kids had to be part of the deal. He always said to me, "Who's going to take care of us when we're old if we don't have kids?" *Oh, I don't know, maybe the robust and thriving second-run-movie-theater community will take us in if some of those Mexican armadillos won't.*

Sometimes Matt and I would sit around the living room on a Saturday night and do our version of telling ghost stories around the campfire. We'd try to imagine what life would be like if we got "the urge."

Well, since we have no family here in California—we could move back to Massachusetts and give up our show business pursuits. Or your mom could move here. Or you could work two jobs while I'm home breast-feeding. Or we could move to a one-room apartment so you wouldn't have to have two jobs and you could stay home and watch me breast-feed.

I admit, when I would see Matt's baby pictures, I'd get some kind of an urge. Those cute dimples. His black curls loose on his head—his head that's a little too big for his baby body. I'd say, "Aw, I long for a Baby Matt." But then I'd head in for snuggles with Adult Matt and realize that dimple is still there; I can run my hand through those curls. I don't want to raise a little Baby Matt. I want to snuggle inappropriately with Adult Matt.

And sure, at times I got offended that Matt didn't seem to have the urge for a Baby Jen running around. How could he not want to make a replica of that girl in the picture who was trying to look so serious and *Swan Lake*-y in her ballet tutu on the front lawn circa 1979? (I was rocking this look long before Natalie Portman made every heterosexual guy in America lust after boobless, boney, and potentially bisexual ballerinas.) Matt reminded me that he'd be a little overwhelmed with his wife *and* daughter in the house, both vying for his attention—after they'd had a glass of wine—because they wanted him to watch them dance and sing along with the movie *Cabaret*.

When I started to think about writing a proposal for this book, I e-mailed Matt to get a quote—in his own words—about his non-paternal instinct. He wrote back, "Jen, please don't e-mail me while you're driving."

I think that's a damn good caretaker instinct, and what girl wouldn't be lucky to have that instinct all to herself?

P.S. I NEVER saw Thomas again except one time on a lunch break at my old temp job. He was leisurely strolling on the other side of the street and looked like he had gained twenty pounds—all of it in his stomach. Maybe he was finally going to have that baby after all.

5. "You'll Change Your Mind"

Throughout my life people have told me that I would "change my mind." I became a vegetarian when I was thirteen and I remember my friend Tracy's mother saying to me at their July Fourth barbecue, "Oh, Jen. This is just a little phase. You'll change your mind." She really thought I'd change my mind, like, that day. She put aside a cheeseburger on a paper plate for me that got rock-hard and cold into the night because I did not change my mind. Twenty-five years later, I'm still a vegetarian. (Okay, I eat fish sometimes. So I guess I'm a pescatarian—or a poseur, or just someone who is committed to not eating anything with legs.)

When I was thirteen my mother told me that I would not always like the music of Morrissey and that someday I'd realize that he "sounds like a British Kermit the Frog." I have seen Morrissey in concert more times in the last three years than I've seen my family on holidays. Not only did I not change my mind about Morrissey, my mom changed *her* mind. She got free tickets to see him perform at Foxwoods Casino and she took a break from playing a slot machine to go check him out. I got a voice mail the next day. "Jennifah, it's Mom. I was front row at Morrissey and wow, is he a crooner or what?" Meanwhile, *I* have never sat front row at a Morrissey concert.

I'm not saying that I've never been wrong about what I want. I'm capable of changing my mind in certain situations and admitting that my judgment was a little off. Like the time in sixth grade when I declared that I was always going to love Ross Damon no matter what and I would never ever change my mind. Then my friend Shannon told me, "Ross Damon put tennis balls in his shorts in gym class today and kept asking everyone to 'touch his balls.'" I changed my mind about Ross immediately. I also once stated that Madonna's song "Borderline" would be my favorite song forever and ever. In my defense, I had no idea that "Vogue" was waiting for me six years down the line.

I said to my dad when I was in high school, "Dad, I don't care about money, only happiness." I'll admit that I've changed my mind on that one. I would like both money and happiness and I'm not entirely convinced that money doesn't buy happiness. I've traveled first class on someone else's dime to Australia, and if you think lying down in a fully reclining seat that turns into a bed while sipping free champagne for eleven hours doesn't solve all of your earthly problems—you're right. But it sure does numb you to the pain of those earthly problems for a little while.

But one thing I haven't changed my mind about is the fact that I am not going to have children. My parents support this decision, yet my choice to be childfree gets questioned by strangers, like they're the CIA and I'm a suspect who isn't giving them the whole story. I wouldn't be surprised if someday one of these baby-happy people decides that in order to get a satisfactory answer, I'll need to be waterboarded on a Slip'N Slide.

MATT AND I were at some mutual friends' wedding in Los Angeles. We were seated with two other couples with whom we were friendly, but we weren't close. Let me put it this way—we were all Facebook friends but we didn't have each other's phone numbers. Somewhere between the breadbasket running out and the salad course being served, one of the other women, let's call her Sally, said to me, "So,

are you and Matt having children?" Sally didn't know she was jump-
ing the gun. Matt and I weren't even married yet at this point, just
newly engaged. The first order of small talk in this situation should
be, "So, are you and Matt having a DJ or a band at the wedding?"
and not, "So, do you two plan to bring a human life onto planet
earth?"

"Oh, we just got engaged," said Matt.

Sally prodded, "Right, but are you two going to have kids?"

You know what? I'm going to refer to her as Lucy, because Sally
was a sweet character from *Peanuts* and Lucy was the know-it-all
character from *Peanuts* who had the gall to open up a psychiatrist
booth without a license, charging five cents to listen to people's
problems.

Matt said, "No." I confirmed our decision, adding, "We don't
want kids."

Lucy wrinkled her nose and cocked her head to one side. Her
voice got high-pitched, like she was really trying to emphasize that
she was asking a *serious* question. "How old are you?" "Thirty-four,"
I answered. Lucy looked at me and with a wave of her hand cleared
the air of the words I'd just spoken. She said, "You don't want kids
now but you're young. You'll change your mind."

I do not like being called "young" by someone who is only a
couple of years older than I am, because what that really means
is "You're dumb." I'm okay with it when elderly people call me
"young." It reminds me that my dread at turning forty is a nonissue.
Forty is still a decade away from menopause. It's like the teen years
of middle age! I especially like when elderly people call less elderly
people "kids." It implies, "Hey, you might be eligible for social
security and discounted movie tickets, but don't think that you've
earned the badge of courage that is known as being 'old' until you
have knee replacement surgery and permanently cold hands. Until
your limbs start breaking from simply trying to open a cabinet and
your grandchildren are kind of afraid of you because you look like
the undead—you're still a kid. Now, who are you and where am I?"

Lucy pressed on. "So, why do you think you don't want kids?" The salads were delivered at this point in the dinner conversation and I realized we had two more courses to go and there was a chance she wasn't going to let up until the cake was cut. I was livid. I had never met her and she was implying in a condescending tone that I only *think* I don't want children? Condescension is not the right tone for wedding small talk with strangers. Condescension is something that should be reserved for conversations with our loved ones or fights with our significant others. What if I was barren? What if this whole "we don't want kids" thing was just a big cover-up because I was too ashamed to say to a total stranger, "My uterus is broken"? What if my fiancé had sperm made out of sawdust and he could never impregnate me? None of this was true, but Loudmouth Lucy didn't know that as she kept poking and prodding away at the status of my uterus, which hurt more than the time that I was physically poked and prodded by my sadistic former gynecologist who insisted that putting two gloved fingers up my butt was now a standard part of my annual Pap smear.

Lucy continued by confiding in me that she and her husband were "trying" to get pregnant. I hate that expression: "We're trying." What that translates to is: "We're fucking." After someone tells me they're "trying," I just get a visual of them having sex without birth control and I don't want to picture other people having sex with or without birth control—unless they are superhot and I am very drunk and have an extra $19.99 to spend on a movie in a hotel room.

When someone tells me, "We're trying," I fantasize about having the following conversation:

"Oh, you're trying? We're trying too. Yeah. It's hard. If you ever need to talk, just call me. There's strength in talking about it—it neutralizes the demons."

"Jen, what are you talking about? I mean we're trying to get pregnant."

"Oh, I thought you meant you were trying not to kill yourselves."

Lucy chomped away at her salad and talked with her mouth full about how at one point her husband, Peter, didn't want to bring kids into the world because he had asthma and was allergic to beets and didn't want to pass down his weak DNA. She said that once they got married their priorities suddenly changed and they wanted to raise children. Matt and I failed to see how our decision to not have kids would change after a ceremony and reception where we'd dance to Kool & the Gang's "Celebration" with our closest friends and family.

Across the table, Matt and Peter started talking and gesticulating wildly about movies—one of those in-depth conversations where guys suddenly sound like they have autism, there is so much attention to detail.

"Matt, you know lots of people think that Orson Welles was the first director to put the camera on the floor, but he borrowed the technique from John Ford, who originally used it in the movie *Stagecoach*."

"Oh yeah, Peter, I knew that! Did you know that Orson Welles secretly watched *Stagecoach* forty times while he was making *Citizen Kane*?"

They couldn't hear what Lucy and I were talking about. If an alien had landed at the table, he would have assumed that Peter and Matt were the married human couple, with the way they'd turned their chairs to completely face each other and how they playfully punched each other in the arm every time the other dork made a really good point about twentieth-century cinema.

"I know you're not even married yet," Lucy lectured, "but at your age, you have to think about making a family *while* you're planning the wedding." Five minutes ago I was too young to know that I was going to change my mind and suddenly I'm too old to waste any time after my wedding to plan on making a family. Which age bracket am I in? Young and stupid or old and barren? And "making a family" is another expression that grosses me out. I pictured Matt standing over me in a lab coat with a turkey baster.

Lucy took a big sip of her red wine, wiped her lip, and leaned into me. She may have been a little drunk or a little dehydrated or a little both, because she had that dry "wine lip" that looked like someone poured purple paint in the cracks of a sidewalk. She leaned in close and whispered, "What would you do if you accidentally got pregnant?" I didn't even understand the question. "Oh, I would never cheat on Matt," I answered. "No, Jen, I mean what if you got pregnant, by accident, with Matt's baby?"

"Are you asking me, someone you barely know, at our friends' wedding, if I would have an *abortion*?"

"Well," she said, "it's something you have to think about if you don't want kids. I mean, I personally think that abortion is something for teenagers who couldn't possibly raise a child. But ever since I decided that I wanted to try to become a mother and I see how difficult it can be to get pregnant, I realize that it's a gift to be pregnant and if a married couple who are both employed accidentally get pregnant, I don't see how you can give that up."

A total stranger tried to small-talk me about abortion. I have never had an abortion. I never want to have an abortion. I also don't want to have a baby. I fear how both procedures would impact my life and leave me full of regret. I didn't lose my virginity until I was twenty. It's not that I'm a prude; I was one of those "I'll do everything but . . ." girls—and no, I don't mean that I did it in the butt. I'd given plenty of blow jobs, and many generous teenage boys had gone down on me on saggy couches in their moms' basements.

After every encounter with oral sex, I was panic-stricken and convinced that I was pregnant. For some reason, despite having taken sex ed class in fifth grade, my perception of how someone gets pregnant grew more and more skewed with each passing year. It got to the point where I was convinced that if I gave a guy a hand job, the sperm would then live on my finger, and since I had forgotten to wash my hands before I peed, the sperm would travel through the thin bathroom tissue when I wiped, jump from the outside of my vagina, and skip up my fallopian tubes. I had the kind of Catholic mom who, I suspected, might withdraw me from school if I got pregnant and make me go upstate, where I would carry the baby to term in some dilapidated mental institution and then give it away to some nice nuns to raise. But I didn't want to leave school and my ballet lessons for nine months. I didn't want to have an abortion either, because when I was sixteen and fearing I was pregnant, I made a promise to God.

I prayed, "God, if I ever get pregnant, I just have to have an abortion. I can't raise a baby. But if I have an abortion, I promise I will become a nun."

I figured I could spend my life being celibate and secretly pining away for boys, writing about them in my diary. It was how I spent my early teen years anyway. As long as nuns could listen to the Cure to help offset some of the loneliness and angst, I was convinced I could handle it. But I was not ready to answer a stranger at a wedding about how I'd handle an accidental pregnancy.

As I stammered and babbled my neurotic tales of teen angst to Lucy, I looked over at Matt and Peter, who were laughing and ordering more whiskey. Why wasn't Matt getting grilled about his supposed immaturity? How was Matt not realizing that I'd been hijacked into a philosophical debate as middle-aged relatives of our friends were starting to drunkenly swipe their fingers through the frosting in the wedding cake? Couldn't he see the SOS looks I was shooting him that said, "Help me. I'm being judged by a woman for an abortion I didn't have!"?

I went to the bathroom and just grabbed on to the sink until my heart stopped racing. I fought back tears. How had I allowed a total stranger to bully me at a fucking wedding? I let the tears fall. Goddamn it! Isn't this why people get engaged, so they don't have to spend Saturday nights crying in bathrooms anymore?

On the drive home Matt and I caught up on the two different conversations we'd had at the wedding.

"Jen, I'm sorry I didn't check in with you. You were talking with your hands and you had plenty of wine in front of you. It seemed like you were having fun."

"Matt, she asked us if we wanted children and then she started whispering at me! What did you think we were talking about?"

"I didn't think about what you were talking about. I was talking to Peter."

"Why can't men think about more than one thing at once? I was talking to Lucy *and* thinking about *your* conversation."

"You win, Jen. You win."

I started talking to Matt like I was his military superior. "Matt, we can't fight. We're on the same side and we have to stay vigilant. This is our new world. People are going to start having kids and I'm not taking the brunt of the pressure. You know what? You need to start lying and saying that you've had a vasectomy."

"I'm not going to lie about things I didn't do to my penis, Jen."

"But that's our trump card! I can say, 'My husband can't make sperm! He paid a doctor to take a knife to his balls! Take that! We *can't* change our minds!"

I thought for sure that once I was in my thirties, people would stop telling me that I was young and that I'd change my mind about not wanting to have children. Someone my age in colonial times would be dead by now, probably from childbirth. "I'm in my thirties" always seemed like a way to say you're in a nice, tidy adult age bracket where you might not yet own a home but you definitely know what you want out of life. I always thought that thirty was that magical age where, just like from Brownies to Girl Scouts, you cross that bridge into the land of Being Taken Seriously as an Adult. I thought that getting married at age thirty-five to a man who also didn't want children would ensure that I finally "won" my own argument. I'm not having children. I was right. Ha. Ha. I didn't change my mind. My eggs are drying up and probably damaged anyway. Even if I did change my mind and wanted to get pregnant at this age, there's a good chance that something would go wrong in the DNA and my baby could end up a Tea Party wacko.

I don't want to wish my life away, but I'm starting to think that life is going to get really sweet when I'm seventy, and people will finally have to accept that I'm old enough to manage my own mind. Although I wouldn't be surprised if someone said, "You say you don't want children but you have early-onset dementia. You only think you don't want kids and you only think that you are presiding over a conversation between your oxygen tank and your St. Francis of Assisi figurine. You'll change your mind."

6. Jesus Never Changed Diapers

Years ago, I was in the women's bathroom at a comedy club in Addison, Texas, after I'd come offstage. (I'm sorry to brag about performing in the suburbs of Texas and using the same bathroom as the audience.) Anyway, I was washing my hands at the sink and a woman came out of the stall. She had seen my set and referenced the part in my act where I talk about how I don't want to have kids, saying she loved my joke that goes: "My husband and I don't want kids. We can't have a third person running around the house who is more helpless than the two of us."

She washed her hands and started to fix her hair in the mirror. "But you want kids someday, right?" she asked.

"Oh! No. I was totally serious. We're . . . childfree by choice," I said, trying to make it sound official, like it was some club I'd joined with a nonrefundable deposit.

She continued to casually fix her hair, reaching into her purse for a trial-size bottle of hairspray and going to work on her Texas bangs. Her gaze remained on herself in the mirror but she said to me, "Really? No kids? So it's just going to be the two of you? Isn't that selfish?"

Do people think that saying the words "Isn't that" in front of "selfish" masks the fact that they just blatantly called me selfish to my face? It's like when people say, "No offense, but," before saying something offensive. Or when someone says, "I don't mean to be racist," and then tells you that they think Puerto Rican people smell like burnt hamburgers.

Isn't that selfish? She'd said it so casually! I'd rather she pulled a combination comb-switchblade out of the back pocket of her jeans, held it up to my neck, and said, "You wanna rumble, you selfish non-child-having bitch? You think you can just go onstage and make jokes and then tell me in a bathroom that you're not interested in bringing a baby into this world? Huh?"

If she were actually *mad* at me about not wanting to have a baby, it would make more sense. I'd know this was just her hot-button issue—she wants everyone to procreate. And I would simply choose to not engage, just like I do with my angry atheist friends who talk about God more than people who believe in one:

"There is no God! It's just something people believe in because they're afraid of death!"

"Okay. So there might not be a God and we're all afraid of death. Well, you've figured that one out. Can we have lunch now?"

"But, Jen, you have to pick a side. You can't just be agnostic. It's as silly as saying you don't know if there's a Santa Claus!"

"Got it. There is no proof of God and it's the parents who put the presents under the Christmas tree. Can we have lunch *now*?"

But it was the way that this woman cemented her bangs to her forehead while she coolly tossed off a judgment about my person that made me realize that whether she was even aware of it or not, somewhere in her core she just assumed that everyone wants to have children, and to *not* want children indicates some sort of factory malfunction. She made me feel like not wanting kids was a character flaw on my part, because I wasn't paying attention in nursery school when we were learning how to share blocks. She could have said any other *s* word. She could have asked, "No kids? Really? Isn't that . . . sexy?" Or, "Isn't that . . . shrewd?" I wouldn't even have bristled so much at being asked, "Isn't that . . . shitty?"

She finished shellacking the top of her head and turned to me to say, "Well, maybe you don't want kids now, but when you're done with all this . . . you might want to give back." And when she said "done with all this," she pointed all five of her fingers at me, like a lazy, droopy version of "talk to the hand." She wiggled her fingers as if to indicate that my career as a stand-up comic, what she called "all this," was something she could lift from me, like a reverse spell.

"It can't be just about you forever, Jen. Trust me. My husband and I couldn't *not* have kids. After a few years of just us, we felt that we were being too . . . selfish. Now I can't even imagine not having brought my daughter into the world. Who was I to keep it from her? Anyway, you're really funny. Good luck with everything!"

And with that unsolicited advice, she matter-of-factly tucked her hairspray back into her purse and walked out of the bathroom, leaving me to stew in the airborne taste of aerosol and that word: "selfish."

I went into a stall and just hid there for a bit, hoping that I wouldn't run into any more women who felt compelled to tell me how funny and how selfish I was. I had to wrap my head around the concept that this woman thought that not bringing her daughter into the world was keeping the world from her daughter. So, every woman who doesn't choose to give birth is leaving some poor kid hanging out there in some kind of limbo? There's a semiexistent child right now holding on to a lottery ticket and he has no idea that his number is never going to come up because he's been assigned to selfish me? Fuck. How do you *stop* having kids with that guilt on your head?

I wanted to run after her and yell, "Hey, I wouldn't have been here making you laugh tonight if I had a baby, because comedians can't take babies on the road!" I thought of adding, "How dare you call me selfish? You were probably at home and your baby threw up on your blouse and you had to change a few times and you said to your husband, 'The girls and I are going out tonight. We just need to laugh!' And I was the one who made you laugh! That's my way of giving back!"

I kicked the tampon receptacle in the stall out of frustration because I came up with the best comeback after she was long gone: *Oh yeah, lady? I'm selfish because I don't have children? Oprah Winfrey doesn't have children and you want to tell me that she's selfish and doesn't give back? She's building schools in Africa and giving away refrigerators that have TVs in them to her audience! She handed Dr. Phil, Dr. Oz, and her best friend, Gayle, their careers and asked for nothing in return! (Except maybe a signed confidentiality agreement or two.) Oprah can afford to have kids and Stedman could stay at home and watch them and she still chooses not to procreate! Why aren't you calling her selfish? And you know who else didn't have kids? Jesus Christ himself! I win! I played the Jesus card! Jesus, the supposed human incarnation of God, who allegedly walked on water, did not have kids. Is he selfish? Didn't he die for our sins or something?* (After fifteen years of going to church every Sunday as a kid, I still don't quite get what that means, but it still sounds pretty unselfish to me.)

One of the casualties of doing stand-up comedy and then using the same bathroom as the audience is that people will talk to you about your act. Sometimes if they like your act, it can be a more difficult conversation to have than if they simply say, "I didn't like you that much." (That happens a lot actually. I get it. I was shouting my opinions into a microphone for almost an hour. People want to tell me their opinions after and sometimes their opinion is that I suck.)

I have a stand-up routine I do about masturbation and the unwanted thoughts that go through women's heads when they put their hands under their sheets. I need a story to think about. I need a fantasy that makes sense. I can't just finger myself and picture Johnny Depp's face. It needs a sense of realism, like how did I meet Johnny Depp? He lives in France. I don't have a work visa. Besides, he has children and I've made it quite clear that I don't want to be a mom and I don't want to be a stepmom either. People love to talk to me about that and share their own tales, which are usually way more graphic than my act. This is part of a conversation that happened between me and a stranger in a women's bathroom at the Improv in Palm Beach, Florida:

> *Are you that comedian who was just up there? No way. I loved your bit about touching yourself. Oh my God, I call it finger blasting! One time I did it in the stall at work. I was so horny. I don't know if it's this new birth control I'm taking or the fact that my husband has been working late and our sex life is a little off. I actually like to rub myself over my underwear. Is that weird? You should put that in your act.*

More power to the woman who finger blasts herself in the bathroom stall at work and then drunkenly confesses it to me. She was just telling me what *she* does without passing any judgment on me, unlike the woman with the *Dynasty* bangs who told me that someday I would definitely want to stop what I do for a living and raise a child.

ONE DAY WHILE I was procrastinating writing this book (okay, looking up how to spell a big word), I was on Dictionary.com and the word of the day was "selfish," with this quote underneath it:

> *The passion of love is essentially selfish, while motherhood widens the circle of our feelings.*
> —Honoré de Balzac

Balzac is a big sack of balls. I know he was an important figure in French literature and some consider him the founder of realism but *fuck you, Balzac.* Is that real enough for you? He wrote this sometime between 1799 and 1850, so becoming a mother was the only thing that women could do back then, unlike today, when women can live a very fulfilling life after making a sex tape, getting a reality TV show, and eventually becoming a human billboard.

　　The way I see it, becoming a mother makes a person selfless in their feelings toward their kid(s) but in a very primal way. It's not even a choice. If a coyote came charging at me, I doubt many of my girlfriends would get on the ground in front of me and let themselves get mauled first, but that's because they didn't make me from their own DNA or adopt me from China after a yearlong process of paperwork and hope.

I'm no Balzac, so what do I know about motherhood? But if a mother's love is selfless, does it mean that all mothers are selfless people toward all of humanity? There's a big difference.

A lot of my friends who had kids in 2008 said that because they were getting no sleep with their new babies, they had no time to pay attention to politics. If someone as seemingly lobotomized as Michele Bachmann can have five children and raise twenty-three foster children while running for president, surely my friends can have one kid and still take the time to make sure that someone like Michele Bachmann never becomes president. Frankly, I think that once you have a child, you *should* take some time out of your day to find out what the people governing our country are planning on doing (or what they say they're planning on doing as opposed to what they are actually doing). How did those pioneer women raise kids and forge across America in caravans in order to start a new life? I don't remember reading in the history books that these women decided that they didn't have time to be part of settling the West because they had to mash up some organic carrots for the baby.

I had other friends who were in a hormonal trance after giving birth and said they just "see things differently now," and with regard to the future of our nation, they put their hands over their ears and sang a chorus of "I can't hear you" because they didn't want to get involved with anything "negative." By the way, I also have friends who say the same thing after doing Ecstasy. Any adjustment to your hormones is going to make you see things differently. Just try to care about global warming after getting fucked really, really good twice in one night.

Becoming a mother doesn't automatically make you a selfless

person. May I present the jury with the following evidence? Kate Moss, Jaid Barrymore, and Brooke Mueller are all mothers. I know, I'm being a little judgmental toward these ladies, but at least I'm not calling them selfish to their faces in a public bathroom! Of course, most people on that list, if they were in a public bathroom, would be bent over the toilet at four in the morning, so it'd be hard to say anything to their faces.

It's simple, really. The urge that most people feel to have kids is the exact same as the urge that I have to *not* have kids. I don't want to have kids and so I am not going to have kids. People who *want* kids are going to *have* kids. I'm doing what I want to do and people who want kids are doing what *they want to do*. What about this scenario makes me selfish? If you did not want to have a baby and yet you found one on your doorstep with a note that said TAKE CARE OF THIS BABY, USING WHATEVER RESOURCES YOU CURRENTLY HAVE, OR EVERYONE ON EARTH DIES, and you chose to sacrifice your life as you knew it so that nobody died, I'd say, "Wow, you are the definition of selfless. Not even Balzac can argue against that."

But if you have enough money to have a kid and you're partnered up with the love of your life and you two want to have children— am I supposed to think that you're doing something more altruistic than I am? It's what you want. It's fun for you. I know that parents skimp on sleep because their kids don't sleep through the night and they need to be fed. I know that some parents work a forty-hour-a-week job in addition to parenting, which is already a more-than-full-time job. Again, no one is making them do it—so I have to assume that the struggle is commensurate with the reward.

My career as a writer, stand-up comedian, and actor is a more-than-full-time job too. Sure, with my jobs, I can take a day off here and there and nobody dies, unlike a parent should she decide, "Nah, I'm not gonna watch my toddler today. I'll check in with him tomorrow if he's around." That doesn't mean that I don't sacrifice or that I'm not sleep deprived, but it's worth it because it's what I want to do to the exclusion of anything else. I do not love the thought of being a mother enough (read: at all) to have a child *and* do what I do for a living. I don't want my spare time, which is an hour here and a weekend there, to be taken up with the making and raising of a person—and I feel like that's the most unselfish thing I can do. I know enough to know what I can't handle—which is a child tugging on my T-shirt and saying, "Feed me," when I walk in my front door. Because usually I'm rushing to the bathroom to pee and you know what? A lot of times I don't make it to the toilet in time and I pee a little bit in my pants. I have my own diapers to change.

I don't go up to parents and say, "You know what you guys should do in addition to what you're already doing? You should start a small charity that helps birds that can't read. What do you mean you don't want to do that? How come you don't want to add that to your schedule? Isn't that selfish?"

I WAS AT a Starbucks on Melrose Avenue in Los Angeles, waiting in line to order an Americano. The woman in front of me had already ordered her coffee but was holding the barista hostage as she and her toddler daughter decided on what the little girl wanted to eat.

"Do you want . . . a cookie? How about a . . . blueberry muffin? Oooh, what about . . . some fruit!"

The toddler, overwhelmed with choices, screamed, "*Noooooooooo!*" to everything. The mom said to the barista, "I'm sorry. Do you have any of those miniscones in the back?" I had about two minutes left on my personal clock to order and get the coffee, otherwise I was going to have to turn around and leave. I didn't want to be late for work. But I'm a pretty patient person for someone who is a complete spaz in all other areas of life and I know that bringing a kid with you into a store with shelves full of goodies turns the simple task of ordering a coffee into an ordeal worthy of rebuilding a community after a devastating hurricane. It involves a lot of bending over, picking things up, and putting them back in their place (reason no. 425 that I don't want kids). The mom turned to me and said, "I'm sorry."

I said, "Oh, it's okay." And then I added, "Being a couple of minutes late for work is worth it for some coffee." I don't know why I said that. I was trying to be funny in that "Hey, we're making jokes about work and coffee" way.

I immediately went into damage control and sputtered, "I didn't mean—"

She cut me off with a look of vague disgust and said, "You don't have kids, do you?" I shook my head no, like I was a toddler who knew I was in trouble and about to get scolded. With a little sneer she said, "It must be nice not having to be responsible for anyone."

Admittedly, I had been silently judging this mom for asking her toddler what she wanted instead of just ordering something, not to mention for her fifteen-hundred-dollar stroller that was more expensive than the first car I drove when I got to L.A. Then I remembered that when I was that girl's age, I sat in my dad's lap and watched TV with him while he puffed on Marlboro Reds. He'd let me play with the smoke swirls. I grew up in the 1970s, before raising kids was thought of as a series of "teachable moments." I'm well aware that I don't know the first thing about how to parent a toddler, but it did seem kind of selfish of this mom to hold up the ever-increasing line.

Once she left Starbucks the guy behind me said, "Hey, we're putting money into the economy and paying taxes that will pay for her kid's public schooling someday." Yes! *Good comeback.* I pay taxes! I do lots of selfless things for other people. In fact, just moments after the whole passive-aggressive joke incident, I tipped the barista one dollar on a two-dollar coffee. That is a 50 percent tip!

I don't understand how busy parents even have two seconds to look over the fence and notice what I'm doing. I couldn't care less what anyone else does about their monthly egg-drop. Have kids. Don't have kids. Be one of those weird adults who like to sleep in a crib and drink from a bottle, pretending they are a kid—whatever gets you through life, as long as you're not harming others, be my guest. It's not like I'm raising babies on a farm and then slaughtering them for food. I'm just not making any babies to start with.

I like to think I'm using all my empathy for good—instead of wasting it on one kid my whole life, I perform selfless, random acts of kindness pretty often for lots of different people. I care about my fellow man and woman and I didn't even birth them! I donate to charities that help children in third world countries get vitamins. I donate to charities that help the environment (your kids can thank me for their clean air once they learn how to talk). I send books to libraries in poor parts of the country. I help support my local food bank with money and canned food. I sign petitions and I call my senators and congresspeople to tell them to stop all of these silly wars that your kids are being forced to fight. I donate clothing to Goodwill every month (without getting a receipt for a tax write-off; you're welcome, America). I actually must be one of the most selfless people on earth because I have no reason to be nice to anyone. I'm not on drugs and I have no maternal hormones pumping through my . . . veins? Brain waves? Arteries? (Where do hormones live?)

One afternoon at CVS, when the woman in front of me realized at the checkout that she'd forgotten her wallet, I purchased the tampons she was trying to buy. I gave my friend a Klonopin once because she wanted to make sure she got some sleep on a flight. No, I'm not a doctor and I guess it's not "legal" to share prescription medication, but my empathy couldn't be stopped. Who doesn't relate to wanting to sleep on a flight?

I used to volunteer at a homeless shelter one Sunday every month. I ultimately had to stop being a Sunday lunch server but it wasn't my fault. I used to talk to this old transient hippie about the Who every time I plopped mashed potatoes on his plate as he made his way down the food line. One day he handed me his phone number and said, "Call me. Or give me your number and I'll call you." First of all—he had a phone? I wanted him to have a phone. But now I wasn't sure whether he was a homeless guy who was starting to make good or just some seventies burnout who came through the line for free hot food and to meet girls. In response to my shocked look he said, "Oh, come on, honey. Don't be a tease."

It would be great if I could use all of the spare time that I have helping others, but it's not that easy. I'd love to be considered unselfish and Christlike, but as a woman it's nearly impossible. Jesus had a penis, so he could feed a homeless person without the dude saying, "Hey, I know phones haven't been invented yet but can I have your number?" Jesus could be nice to strangers without them getting the wrong idea and calling him a tease. And let me remind you once again that Jesus, aka the original Oprah, did not have children either.

7. I Don't Have the Mom Jeans Gene

Aretha Franklin sang, "I didn't know just what was wrong with me / Till your kiss helped me name it / Now I'm no longer doubtful of what I'm living for / 'Cause if I make you happy I don't need no more / 'Cause you make me feel, you make me feel like a natural woman."

That song is not about having a baby, and do you think that anyone dared to get in Aretha's face and tell her that love and kisses are nice but she's not really a natural woman until she pops one out?

I cry. I get manicures and pedicures. I am the sole employee and president of my own corporation. I get my period. I get PMS. I get bloated. I get horny around hot guys. I get horny around quirky-looking guys. I change my hair color and style about four times a year. I think that if I were a lesbian, I'd be a "lipstick" one or I'd like the Hilary Swank–in–*Boys Don't Cry* type. I live alone and am thus the head of my own household. I've had my heart broken. I've broken hearts. Sometimes I feel like I don't have a heart. I've had sex for love and I've had sex for sex. I'm still unsure of my exact bra size. I like how my stomach seems flat in the morning and hate by the end of the day that it resembles a semi-blown-up beach ball half. I have varicose veins that I just don't look at because they're on the backs of my legs. I squeal and clap my hands if a song comes on the radio that I like—even if I've heard it ten thousand times in my life. I do karaoke. I get drunk at weddings. I listen to Madonna. I listen to the Sex Pistols. I've been in therapy for ten years straight. I love my parents and I talk to them on the phone. I yell at my parents when we're on the phone and I just don't have the patience to answer the same question over and over. All of these things make me a woman. I feel pretty natural about it. I don't even own a push-up bra, that's how natural I am. Yet there are people who have tried to invalidate my womanhood because I refuse to do this one thing— grow another person inside my belly.

They act like my not having kids spells the end of the human race. Look, plenty of other women can take care of this. I'd start to get nervous if men were the ones who had to have the babies—*that* would be the end of humanity. My dad cried once because he accidentally used my toothbrush. He hates germs and couldn't fathom how to go on with his life for a good five minutes after the incident. He's a sensitive soul who spends his days trying to avoid physical pain, and using someone's toothbrush could lead to catching a cold, which could lead to a painful sinus headache. So, while I love that women are the ones who got the "people-making equipment," I just don't want to use mine, much like that juicer I have that's still in the box. I simply don't have the urge to make a fresh-squeezed fetus in my lady-blender.

I'm sure squatting in a hole to go number two is actually more natural and the way God intended us to expel our waste—rather than sitting on a porcelain chair and reading the *National Enquirer.* But I'm fine with being unnatural about my bathroom habits. I'm comfortable. Coincidentally, my body is very comfortable not being pregnant. I have some small stretch marks on my inner thigh and I don't know where they're from. I've had them since I was a teenager. I do not write blogs or do interviews with magazines about them, or show them off on TV. There's this cultural fad around women who have stretch marks from pregnancy, claiming that the marks are beautiful and the women are "proud of them." I am not proud of mine. They confuse me. When did I stretch?

Unless your stretch marks have solved a water-shortage crisis or found a way to cap greenhouse gas emissions, let's go easy on the word "proud." Your skin got stretched out because your body went through some changes. There shouldn't be pride in the natural cycle of life. My parents didn't teach me to be overly proud of myself. It's a Catholic thing. (It's also a Massachusetts thing. There's no shortage of people in your family to say, "You think you-ah so great or somethin'? So what you can Hula-Hoop? I saw a boy on TV do it for a wicked long time.") It happens whether we worked hard for our stretch marks or not. And besides, we all know that given the choice, most people would choose to not have stretch marks, unless the reward was sleeping with 1960s Robert Redford. And then you're fucked because he's not going to sleep with you again after he sees those puppies. So let's stop acting like stretch marks are God's greatest gift to women, shall we?

Here's a list of things that don't appeal to me, physically speaking:

- Dying a slow, drawn-out death as the result of an accidental subway incident where I'm trapped between the platform and the train.
- Having any kind of liquid come out of my nipples.
- Having someone bite, tug, chew, and suck on my nipple.
- Shitting in a bed in front of doctors and family.
- Having water break out of my crotch and spill all over the floor.
- Passing a human through my vagina. Or, in an emergency, having a human being cut out of my stomach.

Most of these things can be avoided right now and are within my control. I know that when I'm elderly there will be bed shitting. I'll deal with that when I get there. Maybe they'll invent a Craftmatic Adjustable Bed Toilet by then. The trapped-between-a-train-and-a-subway-platform thing is something I plan to avoid, but a lunatic could always shove me. The other things are *totally* avoidable. I know it all sounds very base when I reduce bringing human life into the world into a series of awkward moments involving bodily secretions, but I can't help it. I'm slightly immature and I often look at things I don't want to do in stark black-and-white terms. It's the most natural thing that a comedian can do.

AFTER MY FIRST year of marriage I gained forty pounds.

I shouldn't say it that way, like I'm blaming the marriage, but everyone I know credited the marriage for my weight gain . . . in a positive way. Friends said, "Well, you found someone and you're happy and you guys are sitting around eating all the time." Or, "Something just happens after you get married; your body starts nesting and just putting on weight." Really? I thought it was because I was eating a block of cheese with my bare hands like a sandwich in front of the TV every night and washing it down with two glasses of pinot noir.

My husband and I had lived together for years before we got married. We'd already gone through our phase of sitting around drinking wine at home together, ordering in, eating out. I didn't gain a single pound. But something about that piece of paper and that ceremony, it's like you're hosting a ritualistic event that you think means one thing, but in fact you're involuntarily letting society—first cousins; friends of your dad's from the Elks Lodge; scheming, jealous, unmarried bridesmaids—put their own spin on it. People always say things like, "I wish I could meet someone so I could have someone to grow old with in forty years." But when you actually get married, they treat you like it's time to start growing old *now*. It's time to gain forty pounds in a year and not even question it. I swear that people were comfortable with my weight gain because it was the closest I was going to get to a baby. Even though I wanted to crawl out of my skin—my friends, family, and total strangers were welcoming me into it. "You're just settling down."

The weight gain snuck up on me. I'm really lucky because when I gain weight I gain it in proportion. I'm glad I didn't inherit my dad's body. He has chicken legs but the stomach of a woman in her third trimester. I don't have a lot of "hangover" on my pants (although I had a lot of hangovers from the pinot noir). I didn't even really notice that I'd gained weight until the first twenty pounds had found their home on my stomach, thighs, and butt. In every photo that I was tagged in on Facebook, it looked like someone had Photoshopped an extra face around my face. I could still button my pants but none of them were fitting in the crotch anymore. That area went beyond looking like I had camel toe—it looked like one of those Pillsbury Crescent rolls that during its baking period starts to explode and grow a deformed bread buddy that rides sidecar on the original. I wondered, *Did nobody tell me that after age thirty-five a woman's balls drop?* I started saying things about those pants that I could no longer pull up ("They don't make them like they used to!"), even though I'd had the pants for years and at one time they fit perfectly. It's not like a pack of tailor-elves had been coming into my room at night, saying, "Hey, they're not making pants like they used to! The store sent us here to change the inseam."

I couldn't even really wear Spanx anymore. The Spanx weren't strong enough to suck anything in. It was just a bunch of stretchy material that sat between my skin and my clothes, adding another sixteenth of an inch of fabric to my all-over bulge. I was a new woman. I was round and on my way to Rubenesque. There's nothing wrong with that, of course, but I've always been mindful of my weight. (Although I've never been anorexic or bulimic—mostly because the only thing worse than feeling hungry is the feeling of throwing up, so I'm not a good candidate for either disorder, but also because I'm lazy. I can't add calorie counting or hiding vomit around the house to my already packed schedule of procrastinating.) And because I took ballet every weekday for almost thirteen years, I was naturally skinny. I ate Pop-Tarts and ice cream after dance class every day and didn't gain a pound. I know, I hate people who say that they can eat whatever they want and not gain weight. But don't hate me, that metabolism stopped when leg warmers went out of style.

I didn't have enough body fat to get my period when everyone else did. Every girl wants to get her period because we're told that it means we are "women." All getting your period really means is that now you can get pregnant—and as we've seen from all of these reality shows about teen moms, these girls can barely be considered women. Female, yes, but what does that even mean anymore? The Pregnant Man used to be "all-female" and having a baby didn't make him any more of a woman.

Getting your period is also the beginning of an approximately forty-year stretch where once a month you don't feel like having sex or wearing white pants. And in the sixth grade all of the other girls were becoming "women" all around me. My mom had a box of maxi pads in the cabinet under our bathroom sink. I used to hope that just touching it would signal my body to start shedding my uterine lining and I'd be on my way to walking carefree on the beach in a white linen dress, just like the woman on the box. I didn't hit "womanhood" until I was fourteen years old. And once I did—all I wanted was to run back to girlhood and not have to wear what seemed like a small neck pillow between my legs five days out of the month.

My postmarriage weight gain forced me into a new daily uniform: stretch pants with a beach cover-up/tunic that covered my butt and the tops of my thighs. It was comfortable and I never had to face the reality that my skin didn't fit into my usual clothing. Stretch pants and beach cover-ups are enablers. They'll never tell you the truth like a pair of jeans that won't go up your thigh. Stretchy clothing will accommodate you no matter how heavy you get, with no regard for your health. The fabric just hangs on you like your alcoholic friend who needs to get sober and gets mad at you when you say that you want to cut down on your drinking.

When I told my closest friends how much weight I'd gained, they all lied to my face and said, "Really? I can't tell. You must hold it really well. Maybe this is a good weight for you." But I knew the truth. Whenever I was about five pounds over a weight that was comfortable to me, I'd run to Weight Watchers. A few times when I would check in, the woman behind the counter would say, "You know you're at a healthy BMI—but I can't turn you away since technically you're not underweight." She'd hand me my punch card back and sort of look at me disapprovingly. But lately at Weight Watchers meetings, they punched my card, smiled big, and said, "Welcome!" And every time I weighed in—showing that I'd not lost a pound—they'd make a sad face and commiserate: "It's hard, isn't it?" If Weight Watchers was welcoming me without a disclaimer—I knew. I was officially chubby. And even worse? Not famous enough to get an endorsement deal while I counted those points.

I wanted to lose this postmarriage weight. I'd had to move all of my clothes to a spare closet in the hopes that one day my plus-size crotch could fit into all of my pants again. Being overweight made me feel sad. When I'm sad I eat, then I feel fat and that makes me sad, so I eat more. It's a vicious (but fun) cycle.

I've always been a healthy person. I've been a vegetarian since I was thirteen years old. Sadly, I wish it were because I was committed to ending the slaughter of innocent animals, but it's because Morrissey from the Smiths is a vegetarian, because *he* is committed to ending the slaughter of innocent animals. A few months after I got married, I was the healthiest-eating person who waddled you'd ever met. I was eating healthy foods *and* six pieces of pizza a day. If one day passed when I'd managed to avoid sugar and bread, I'd get on that scale and if I hadn't dropped ten pounds, I'd grow frustrated and drink three smoothies to soothe myself about how hard it is to lose weight in one day. Don't judge! Those smoothies had vitamin C and açai berry!

I tried to motivate myself into working out again by going to bed at nine o'clock and setting my alarm for six with every intention of going jogging around my neighborhood. Every morning I'd wake up cranky to the sound of my alarm and violently hit snooze. I'd feel insulted, condescended to—as if the alarm had set itself because it noticed I'd gotten a little chunky. I'd think, *It's still dark outside. Not even farmers are awake this early. It's dangerous to be up this early—this is when all of the murderers are just finishing up their rounds for the night and they have time for one more quick alley-strangling before they go to bed at sunrise.*

I'd put on my gym clothes around five o'clock at the office so that I could stay in the mind-set of "going to the gym after work." *Well, the gym clothes are on, so it's not like I'm going to get into my car and just drive by the gym.* And every night at six, I'd get in my car wearing workout clothes and . . . just drive by the gym and head home.

Eventually I got tired of wearing wrap dresses, because every day in the kitchen at work I'd run into someone who would say, "You're dressed up today! You have big plans tonight?"

"No," I'd answer. "I just don't have any pants that fit."

"Oh, Jen. You're so funny."

"No. I'm serious. I'm not going anywhere tonight. I'm going home to stand around and feel my thighs touching."

I decided that until I lost the weight, I at least had to wear a pair of jeans that fit. I'd seen billboards for a brand of jeans called Not Your Daughter's Jeans that promised to suck your stomach in up to your neck. Until now, I'd resisted putting something called Not Your Daughter's Jeans on my body. It's a wildly insulting name when you think about it. It's nothing like that Oldsmobile ad campaign from the 1990s: "It's Not Your Father's Oldsmobile." That meant, "Your dad isn't that cool but you are. We have updated, cool Oldsmobiles for you, you young, hip person." Not Your Daughter's Jeans implies, "Oh, your daughter wouldn't wear these jeans. They're for older, heavier women. Your daughter is a size zero. She doesn't put peanut butter on a doughnut and call it a high-protein breakfast.

Your daughter doesn't need to wear a body shaper with sweatpants. Men want to have sex with your daughter and not you." Not Your Daughter's Jeans abbreviates their brand to NYDJ in a lot of their ads. I guess they're hoping people get confused and think, *Oooh, NYDJ. That must be the brand of jeans that cool New York disc jockeys wear.*

I went to a mall to try to find some Not Your Daughter's Jeans and one of these young "daughter types" was working the counter. She said to me in that baby voice that's all the rage nowadays, "Um, no? We don't have that brand? But why don't you buy the jeans you used to wear but a few sizes bigger?" Yeah, why don't I go to Home Depot, buy some rope, and hang myself? I know my options.

I left the mall without the NYDJ jeans, but I treated myself to a frozen yogurt because I felt I'd earned it after walking and standing for thirty minutes in a row.

The people who will tell you the truth in this situation are gay guys and your mom. I don't really have any gay guys in my life anymore. (I have a theory that gay guys are closer with straight women when they're both at a period in their lives when they realize that they like penises but aren't quite sure how to go about interacting with them. Once gay guys come out, it's just a constant hunt for dick, working out at the gym, and buying dog beds. The straight-girl friend isn't coming over for any more Friday-night sessions of singing into a hairbrush to En Vogue's "My Lovin' [You're Never Gonna Get It].")

But it took a gay guy to make me realize that my stomach full of burritos looked like a baby.

I was at a happy hour with a friend. We were standing around chatting when a gay man-friend of hers came running over. It was pretty loud already (we were in a gaycentric restaurant, so it's always a nightclub no matter what time of day). Natasha introduced me to her friend and said, "This is Jen. She just got married this year!" The *oontz-oontz* of the bass was too loud for him to hear her correctly, but he could tell that a woman was standing in front of him and another woman was excited for her and there was news. He shrieked in support and you didn't need a quiet bar to hear the international language of "someone thinks you're fat." He put his hand on my stomach and said, "Congratulations! When are you due?" I wanted to go back to my local senior center and undo my vote in support of gay marriage.

MY MOM GETS to see me on television about once a week on *Chelsea Lately*. She'd been at home reclining in her chair over the past few months and noticing that her daughter Jen's normally pointy chin was becoming very round. She thought to herself, *This is beyond the camera adding ten pounds. I wonder if Jen is pregnant. She's been married for seven months. She could be.*

One day, I was sitting in my Spanx and eating my second bagel of the day in my office, e-mailing with my older sister Violet, who is also a member of the childfree-by-choice club. (She has three cats, a pony, and two horses; she prefers her living, breathing responsibilities to have fur, a shorter life span, and no need for a college education.)

I waddled away from my desk to head to the kitchen for a third bagel and I forgot to lock my computer. I left my Microsoft Outlook open. Chelsea walked into my office and composed an e-mail to my sister.

Violet, I'm pregnant. We didn't want to have kids. It's a mistake. I'm not sure if I'm going to keep the baby. I want to talk to Mom about options. But you have to tell her. So call her on my behalf tonight.

Chelsea walked out of my office. I waddled back into my office. The only thing I saw was an e-mail from my boss Sue, telling us we could go home early. I shut down my computer, never checking my sent messages. I stopped by the kitchen to grab a fourth bagel for the ride home. My cell phone started ringing during my commute. It was Violet. I was driving, so I ignored it—I was too busy singing along to

Juice Newton's "Angel of the Morning" in between bagel bites. My sister calls me a lot and usually she doesn't even want me to pick up, she just wants to narrate *The Bachelor* into my voice mail. "Jen? It's Violet. What's up? Oh my Gawd this girl is such a geek. She's cryin' because she didn't get picked to go on the helicoptah ride."

I went to bed that night having never called Violet back. In the morning, I listened to her messages.

> First message: "Jen, I got your e-mail. What the hell is going on?" I was still waking up and thought, *What the hell* is *going on? What e-mail?*
> Second message: "Jen, you're pregnant? You really want me to tell Mom? Let's at least talk first."
> Third message: "Jen, I called Mom. I couldn't bring myself to tell her but I did tell her that you have something to tell her. So call her this morning."

I called Violet and she read me "my" e-mail to her. She believed me when I told her that Chelsea wrote the e-mail, but convincing my mom that nothing was wrong would be another story. I bit the bullet, called my mom, and said, "So, Violet told you I have something to tell you?"

My mom couldn't stop the panic in her voice: "Jennifah, what is it? Is something wrong in yah marriage?"

"No, Mom. Everything is fine. Listen, Chelsea broke into my computer and e-mailed Violet, telling her I was pregnant."

The panic in my mom's voice shot off like a rocket: "Jennifah, you're *pregnant*?"

"No. I'm not pregnant. Chelsea was playing a prank."

"Well, Jennifah, why would she do that if you're not pregnant?"

"Mom. Do you know what a prank is? You don't spread truths about someone if you're pranking them. She was kidding. This conversation that you and I are having now is exactly what Chelsea wanted to have happen."

My mom's rocket tumbled back to earth and now her voice was somber. "But you really ah pregnant, aren't you?"

And she was off and running before I could even get a word in. "You know this is so funny, Jennifah, because I was watching you on TV the othah night and you know I think you're a beautiful girl but your face is so round. It's just like a pregnant woman. You look like you-ah filled with water, like a balloon . . ."

"Mom!"

"Oh, Jennifah, what ah you gonna *do*?"

So my mom had just done two things that are probably not in any handbook called *A Normal Parent's Reaction to Things*. First, she lamented that her married, thirty-five-year-old daughter might be pregnant. Typically moms are laying a guilt trip to convince their thirty-five-year-old married daughters to *have* children. I've always thought that mothers who ask their children to provide them with grandchildren are acting like Joe Francis, the mastermind behind *Girls Gone Wild*: *Come on! Take your top off for the camera because it will benefit me!* It disturbs me on one level that suddenly, marriage invites people's parents into the bedroom. At a certain point, we all have to admit that parents asking their children for grandchildren is really just a polite way of parents asking their kids to get down and fuck. *Come on, honey! Take your pants off and let my son-in-law penetrate your vagina without a condom. I know I raised you to be modest but I must ask you, just this once, to put a pillow under your butt and get those legs up over your head so that when he ejaculates his sperm inside of you, it just slides right into your uterus and makes me a grandchild on the first night of your honeymoon!*

Second, my mom essentially confirmed that the camera had added its magical ten pounds to the twenty pounds that I'd added to myself and I looked like a human water balloon.

I stood outside of a Starbucks, shouting into my BlackBerry, "Mom, don't worry, I'm not pregnant!" as people stared while making awkward attempts to hold the door for me. It was like the opposite of the conversation that Madonna had in her song "Papa

Don't Preach." I wasn't in trouble deep and I was not going to keep my baby—because there wasn't one.

I'M NOT MAKING fun of my mom and I'm not just saying that because she's going to read this. I wouldn't have it any other way. I love having a mom who, if I were pregnant, would automatically ask, "But what about your career?"

There's an article tacked to my corkboard that my mom ripped out of a magazine. The headline is "Child-Free by Choice" and the byline is "Not sure motherhood's for you? You're not alone." My mom wrote on a Post-it note:

This is from an old magazine that I found in a drawer. However, I think it's still relevant.

The note is written in her perfect Catholic school–taught cursive handwriting. In addition to writing in perfect cursive, my mom is the last of a generation who still clips articles and sends them via snail mail when she could just e-mail them to me. I appreciate it, though, because my e-mail account is already clogged up with friends from high school who have turned ultraconservative and send me forwards about how illegal immigrants are bringing down the economic system and stealing all of our jobs.

My mom is really supportive of my decision/instinct not to have a kid. Part of me thinks the fact that I'm publishing a book about it makes her even more supportive. Even though I know her support is genuine, I think that if I decided to become a Wiccan transsexual poet, the acceptance of that would come easier if there was a promise of a book display at Barnes and Noble stores nationwide of *Jen Kirkman: My Life as a Wiccan Transsexual Poet*, and a possible appearance on *The View*.

She told me recently that I never played with baby dolls as a kid.

"In fact, Jennifah, you took the clothes off a baby doll I bought you and instead dressed up the cat like a woman and then did a photo shoot. You had a Cabbage Patch doll named Ramona whom you loved, but I think it was because she was named aftah those books you liked. And Cabbage Patch was more of a status symbol anyway. You usually carried her by the arm and let her yahn hair drag on the floor."

(This further supports my theory that the childhood signs that you have no instinct to mother *anything*, not even cats or dolls, are very similar to the signs that you will grow up to be a gay man—both evident before age ten.)

My mom kept interrupting the stories about me to tell me about herself: "Jennifah, I never thought to say, 'Why don't you be a moth-ah when you grow up?' I thought it would take away from what you were showing me you wanted to do. All you did was talk about show business. When you weren't at ballet and tap school you were putting on shows in the living room for nobody. Everywhere I took you, you asked people if you could tap-dance for them."

To be honest, it sounds like I was an annoying kid. Thirty years later, whenever I'm drunk, if there is a DJ in the vicinity, I request "Thriller" and I do an interpretative dance. (This half-serious dance is to distract from the fact that I can't quite nail those Michael Jackson/zombie moves.) A lot of people, when they drink, their hometown accents come out. When I drink, my inner child comes out and all I want to do is dance for you. Thank God this (usually) happens when I'm hanging out with other drunken people who hopefully just think that I'm standing still and it's the room that's spinning.

At the end of our phone call outside Starbucks, my mom finally believed that I was not pregnant and that I wouldn't be having an abortion or a baby. But she also reminded me that no matter what happened—if I did end up having a baby sometime—she would support me and not judge.

My mom's only regret about my plan not to have children has to do with her desire to look at potentially beautiful people. When I interviewed her for this book, she said to me, "Jennifah, I think your children would be beautiful and it sometimes makes me sad that I won't get to look at attractive children who you made. That's what moth-ahs think. Don't let anyone tell you differently. It's not always some altruistic thing. Sometimes you just think your children are so good-looking that you want to see more of them."

That's what I love about my mom ever since she's entered her seventies. She's still lucid but has the honesty of someone who's lost her mind. I'm up to my neck in hearing my friends listing their reasons for having kids, how it's all about "taking part in creating the next generation" and "carrying on the species" and "giving back." I appreciate that my mom admitted on behalf of all mothers that what drives procreation for the most part is the desire to see what the combined genes of you and your spouse would look like. If I want to see what another man and I could create, we'll just take a walk down to the Venice Beach boardwalk and have someone draw our caricatures.

It took a year but I finally got my preburrito body back and lost thirty pounds. It involved actually moving my limbs and walking and not eating four bagels every morning for breakfast—oh, and getting a divorce . . .

8. Faking It for George Clooney

Having children has had an enormous effect on me as a person, and creatively. When you have children you look at life differently. You have a much fuller sense of appreciation for the fragility of life, and how magical we all are as human beings.

—Madonna

Oh, Madonna. You claim to have had a cabdriver drop you off in Times Square with only fifty dollars in your pocket when you first moved to New York City in the 1970s. Then you became the biggest pop star in the world. You married Sean Penn and you introduced us all to Vogueing. While you were doing all of that, I was so painfully aware of the fragility of life that I had to be put on Prozac to calm my anxiety. Now that my serotonin levels are evened out, I don't need a kid to remind me again about the fragility of this life. Also, I think you realized how magical life was before you had kids when you sang in "Like a Prayer," "Life is a mystery / Everyone must stand alone / I hear you call my name / And it feels like home," and then made out with that hot, black Jesus.

The nail salon is a place where small talk breeds like Michelle and Jim Bob Duggar. (His name is fucking *Jim Bob* and he has nineteen kids. If I invented a character named Jim Bob who bred nineteen people, any television network executive or movie studio mogul would say, "That sounds a little clichéd. I mean is anybody *really* named Jim Bob? Even we hateful Hollywood writers can admit that's a name that's manufactured by the likes of us who still harbor contempt for our flyover-state hometowns.")

At a nail salon, when a woman whom you've never met looks over and asks, "What color is that you're getting?" that's one degree of separation away from, "Do you have children? Let's talk about our kids!" It's a strange phenomenon, but when mothers have an hour to spare, they want out of the house and away from their kids—and yet they can't stop talking about them. Mom's manicure is just going to get fucked up right when she gets home, when Billy hands her an action figure wrapped in a hard-to-open plastic package and says, "Get this out for me, Mommy, or I will start screaming like Mel Gibson about the Jews and you'll rue the day you left me at home and went to a nail salon!" But she wants out of the house anyway just so she doesn't have to listen to inane cartoons or talk in a baby voice for sixty minutes. She can sit down and have a real, adult conversation about . . . babies.

Women who have babies have these predictable hormones that make it impossible for them to talk about anything but babies. Just like every teenager has predictable hormones that make them so horny that they'll dry-hump a throw pillow to orgasm.

New moms especially have that glazed-over Heaven's Gate look in their I-had-to-stop-taking-Xanax-while-breast-feeding eyes.

Remember when Katie Holmes started (contractually) dating her (benefactor) boyfriend Tom Cruise? She couldn't stop saying, "Tom is amazing. Everything is amazing." I'm sure everything *was* amazing for Katie at first—until she filed for divorce seven years later. I remember reading that on their first date, Tom flew Katie on a private jet to Paris for dinner. I'm not sure whether he took control of her brain on board the flight or under the Eiffel Tower, but she definitely wasn't in Dawson's Creek anymore. Once Tom started having

Scientology minders follow Katie around (I know these things; I read *Star* magazine) and he changed her name to "Kate," I'm sure there were moments when Katie/Kate/Mrs. Cruise thought, *Oh my God. What the fuck have I done? I'm not myself anymore. But I'm the one who wouldn't shut the fuck up about how amazing everything was and I'll look stupid if I suddenly change course now and say, "It was amazing but now it's just like every other relationship, full of challenges and compromise and not all that glamorous." Well, I'm just going to keep saying "amazing" because there's no turning back. And every time I do literally turn back, there is someone on Tom's payroll following me. It's amazing!*

This is what new moms remind me of. (Although on a side note, I have to admit, even though I'm convinced that she's part robot, I'm completely taken with Suri Cruise. She wears high heels and lipstick and walks around Manhattan carrying a Starbucks cup and she's six years old. She doesn't play with other kids and although that sounds sad on paper, think of all the germs she's avoiding. You never see a picture of Suri Cruise with a summer cold. If I had to have a kid, I'd want Suri Cruise. She could totally get me in to see all of the cool shows at Fashion Week and I'd probably get a pretty sick allowance.)

New moms love to start conversations with strangers like the one I had with my manicurist "Tammy" when I was still married. I didn't put her name in quotations to protect her identity. The tag was too small for, "We all know this woman's name is something you could never pronounce and she doesn't want to hear you butchering her native tongue, so she picked one of your boring American names so that you people can address her. You happy? *Tammy.*"

Tammy noticed my wedding ring as she removed my chipped nail polish and asked, "Do you and your husband have children?"

That day I replied no with confidence. I used to answer that question, "Naaaaww," with a song in my voice because I was trying to sound pleasant and not like some emotionally closed-off Anti-mother Monster who stomps through neighborhoods, lifting roofs off homes, grabbing children out of their cribs, and actually gnawing off their cheeks and toes, unlike most adults, who just jokingly threaten to do so.

I'm not an emotionally closed-off Antimother Monster but that seems to be how people with kids see me, so I used to say, "Naaaaww," hoping that it would read as, "Awwww, I just don't want kids but I'm supersweet and I'm happy to hear your stories about kids. I think it's funny, for example, when a toddler's first words are 'Goddamn it.' You have kids. I don't. Different strokes for different folks! What a wonderful world! Awwww. Naaaaww."

But despite my best efforts, never once has answering, "Naaaaww," ever been met with a simple, "Oh. Okay."

So this time when I answered no, I didn't smile. I didn't maintain eye contact. I did nothing to indicate that this topic—or any topic for that matter, Tammy—was on the table for dissection. I put my nose back into my book. But I might as well have chucked the book into my bucket of foot-soak, pulled out an accordion, played a tune, and sung, "Ask me anything!" because Tammy didn't pick up on my social cues.

She stopped filing my nails. She grabbed my hand and forced my eyes to meet hers. She said, "In my country, it is against the family and your husband to not want to give them a child. It is a sin."

I wanted to say, "Well, that sounds oppressive. So aren't you glad you're no longer living in that country with your no-fun family?" Instead, I said, "Well, my relatives and my husband are fine with my decision." Tammy admonished me, "When it's too late you will want one and then you will have no eggs left." Oh, okay, I didn't realize that it was Buy One Manicure, Get a Fucked-Up Fortune of Doom Day.

I regularly tip more than 20 percent in cash at this place and in my humble opinion that means that I should not have to be lectured about adopting the sexist rules of a third world country that I never intend to eat food from, let alone visit. It's bad enough that during my manicure I have to inhale the acrylic nail fumes from the Real Housewife of the Cheaper Neighborhood Five Miles from

Beverly Hills who's sitting next to me, incense from the Buddha shrine in the doorway, and unattended burnt rice from the Crock-Pot in the bathroom. Besides, when someone is rubbing lotion on my feet and legs as if they're trying to seduce and make love to me—I don't think there should be any conversation at all. Focus!

I WENT BACK to that nail salon recently with two fewer accessories: my wedding and engagement rings. I walked in and Tammy, who had once casually informed me that I was dishonoring my mother and father, smiled and greeted me with, "We missed you! Welcome back." Either I'd made quite the good impression on her last year despite my failure as a woman, or she thinks that all white girls look alike.

I took a seat and held an *Us Weekly* magazine in front of my face. I don't know what's worse: being told by a manicurist that in her country not becoming a mother is a pox on the family, or having my intelligence insulted with the term "baby bump." When a woman is pregnant and her belly protrudes—what you're seeing is a baby. Not a baby bump. A baby bump is a worrisome growth on your baby that needs to be surgically removed. I remember that when celebrities used to talk about "bumps," they were whispering in the bathroom at the Chateau Marmont on the Sunset Strip about doing a little cocaine. Actually, I don't personally remember that. I've never been a celebrity, a drug user, or a bathroom attendant at the Chateau. But now, "bump" no longer refers to a thing that makes you stay up all night and talk fast. "Bump" refers to a thing that makes you stay up all night and breast-feed.

At least one double-page spread in any celebrity gossip magazine is dedicated to baby bumps (real ones or false-alarm celebrity bloating). I did some pretty intense research on the origin of the term "baby bump." I typed "baby bump origin" into Google and clicked on the first result. According to a *Washington Post* article from 2008, "the term appears to be British in origin and in use." I'm mad at

Britain now. They gave my parents the Beatles but their export for my generation is the expression "baby bump"?

There's a Baby Bump Watch in most issues of *In Touch*, *Us Weekly*, and *InStyle* magazines. Photographers and editors are on the case! No pregnant celebrity will be able to wait the requisite twelve weeks to announce her pregnancy anymore! The Baby Bump Watch Patrol will make sure that every time you leave the house holding your purse suspiciously at uterus level, wear an empire-waisted-dress, or have yet to digest a high-carb lunch, you will be up for the very public debate of "Is She or Isn't She?"

I'm just waiting for there to be an Adoption Papers Bump Watch that analyzes photos of celebrity women who carry overstuffed attachés filled with what seem to be reams of legal documents. "Is She Adopting or Is She Working Part-Time as a Paralegal?"

While I waited for Tammy to start in on my manicure, I read about how January Jones eats her own placenta. I removed the spoonful of vanilla frozen yogurt from my mouth and pushed the cup aside.

January Jones informs us: "Our placenta gets dehydrated and made into vitamins. It's something I was very hesitant about, but we're the only mammals who don't ingest our own placentas." We're also the only mammals who can pay doctors to throw our placentas in human wastebins and then walk to a pharmacy and pick up bottles of vitamins that produce the same health benefits as our human postbaby slime.

The idea of someone eating her own placenta makes me think of a woman with a lobster bib around her neck, picking up a sloppy, goopy, jellyfish mound of wetness. It falls through her fingers and she tries to quickly shove it into her mouth. Ironically January Jones plays Betty Draper on *Mad Men*—a housewife from the 1960s who would not even be allowed to say the word "pregnant" if she were a character on a TV show. (In the 1950s, the CBS network wouldn't allow Lucille Ball's character, Lucy, to refer to herself as pregnant and so in the episodes where she was carrying Little Ricky, the network censors insisted that she say "expecting.")

I don't want to go back to the days when "pregnancy" was a bad word, but maybe we can agree that while I'm trying to relax and eat some frozen yogurt at the nail salon, I don't need to read about Hollywood stars ingesting their own placentas? That's what online fetish websites are for—people who want to think about goo on an actress's face in the privacy of their own home.

Granted, placenta is probably great for your health. Like colonics. Sometimes I get colonics but I'd never take to a magazine to let everyone know that one time my fecal matter was shaped like a hook, preventing it from passing through my intestines properly. When I lay in that bed and saw my hooklike poop swim through the colonic machine, I never felt so in touch with my body. Do you know we are the only mammals who need to pay people to stick tubes up our asses and flush us with water to help us shit? We are! It's such a miracle!

See? How do you like it? It's gross. You owe me a frozen yogurt, January Jones.

IT REALLY SEEMS like over the past few years babies have replaced pashminas as the hot new accessory to drape your arms around. Maybe my resistance to having a baby has something to do with my natural resistance to look like everyone else or to do what the magazines dictate. My mom didn't allow me to wear Guess jeans in 1986. "Jennifah, all the girls wear those. Why do you want to look like everyone else?" Instead, she just outfitted me in the Wrangler version of Guess jeans so that I could look like the slightly worse-off version of everyone else. Now that I think of it, I'm sure my mom knew full well she was just trying to save money but realized she could couch her thriftiness in a morality lesson. I don't think her main aim was to cultivate in me a sense of individuality, because when I started wearing thrift-store black dresses, ripped tights, and combat boots and dyeing my hair jet black, her tune changed to, "Jennifah, why can't you wear some color? It's very much in style right now. You look like a witch with shoe polish on her head."

I switched to another magazine that was a few months old. If the World Wide Web ever permanently crashes and I need to know who won the Oscars in 2009—I think the nail salon would be the first place I'd go to find out. The windowsill at any given manicure place is like a national archive of celebrity gossip. I don't know what happens to the new magazines. I have a feeling that Tammy and her cohorts take the new ones home and keep them on the back of the toilet, where they are left to absorb foul odors and humidity that makes the pages curl, only to bring them back to the salon six months later.

I read that Jay-Z made some big changes in his career upon the birth of his new daughter, Blue Ivy. (By the way, whenever I hear that name I can't help but think of the late porn star Blue Iris, who was a frequent guest on Howard Stern's radio show. I hope for the best for Jay-Z's baby and that she doesn't grow up to become a granny who says, "I'm getting myself hot," and shows her elderly gray pussy on Pay-Per-View.)

Jay-Z had allegedly decided that since he has a daughter, he would no longer say the word "bitch" in any of his songs. He even supposedly released a poem promising as much:

> *Before I got in the game, made a change, and got rich*
> *I didn't think hard about using the word bitch*
> *I rapped, I flipped it, I sold it, I lived it*
> *Now with my daughter in this world I curse those that give it.*

Unfortunately, before I could get all huffy and wonder whether Hova ever considered the feelings and opinions and struggles of his mother, his wife, and his female friends *before* his daughter was born, the report was exposed as a hoax. Apparently there are still plenty of bitches in his life that he holds near and dear and it did not take making a baby for him to have basic empathy and a social conscience. Jay-Z, I salute you.

But so many other celebrities who are not married to Beyoncé claim that until they had a baby their lives were just a series of trivial things like maintaining a movie career, and now that they have a baby their lives have real meaning. I've never had a movie career or a baby and I'm a firm believer that my life has a lot of meaning! I believe that every person on earth has meaning just by being alive. I also believe that the meaning of life is to love—whether you love a child or a string of skinny-jeans-wearing bass-player boys. One of my favorite quotes about the meaning of life is from American contemporary spiritual leader Ram Dass: "We're all just walking each other home." I'd never have known he said this if I weren't scrolling through Twitter, but whatever, it still counts as spiritual reading.

Even though I don't have a maternal instinct, I often fantasize about helping some of these celebrity babies that I read about in *Us Weekly's* "Toddlers—They're Just Like Us" section.

Me: "Hey, I'm worried about you."

Celebrity Baby: "Who are you?"

Me: "Oh, just a nosy person who keeps reading about you and your family in the tabloids."

Celebrity Baby: "I'm in a magazine? People can see my picture and know what I look like? What if someone decides to kidnap me? I'll be so easy to find!"

Me: "I know. I don't know if your parents have the best judgment. They're kind of using you to prove to the world that they're not complete narcissists. Not that the definition of 'narcissist' is 'childfree.' It actually just means an inability to feel empathy. Lots of childfree people are still quite empathetic, usually not toward children but . . . I feel bad for stuffed animals in stores that no one buys. That counts as selfless."

Celebrity Baby: "My parents seem nice, although I still don't get why I'm white and my mom is Mexican."

Me: "Oh, no, honey. That's not your mom. That's your nanny."

Celebrity Baby: "Oh. Where's my mom?"

Me: "She's off filming a movie in Vancouver for a few
months."

Celebrity Baby: "But I thought her life had meaning when I was
born and that movies weren't that important. So why is she
making more?"

Me: "Well, it *is* her job."

Celebrity Baby: "But she has dozens of millions in the bank and
owns four estates all over the world. I didn't think she had
to work."

Me: "Look, I told you they have judgment problems. Your parents seem to think that birthing you or paying their surrogate to birth you because they were too busy not wanting
to get fat has transformed them into good people who suddenly understand the meaning of life and now care about
things outside of themselves."

Celebrity Baby: "But do I count as something outside of themselves? I mean, technically I am an extension of them. Who
wouldn't want a cute miniversion of herself and her hot
actor husband?"

Me: "You seem pretty smart for your age."

Celebrity Baby: "Yeah, well, I have to be pretty smart for my
age, don't I? I just found out that my parents didn't have a
basic moral code until I was born. They sound pretty fucking stupid if you ask me. Besides, why aren't my parents
filming movies in Los Angeles? One of our greatest exports,
Hollywood, is being outsourced to Canada. This is why our
economy is in the shitter."

Next in my trashy-magazine-a-thon, I happened upon this quote
from Sarah Jessica Parker:

As a working mother high heels don't really fit into my life any-
more—but in a totally wonderful way. I would much rather think
about my son than myself.

Have these moms ever heard of yoga? Meditation? Volunteering for the elderly or the homeless? Taking care of a relative? There are *lots* of ways to not think about yourself and when you've truly mastered not thinking about yourself, you don't even have the urge to tell everyone that you are not thinking about yourself!

You know who does a lot of good deeds and doesn't have kids *and* totally understands what's important in life? George Clooney. Unlike me, he doesn't give a fuck what you think about the fact that he's not "selfless" enough to father a kid. He's not writing a book defending his position. He's having sex with a cocktail waitress and then saving Darfur. Both are noble positions.

I read in *Marie Claire* that George said, "Even one kid running around my villa makes me nervous, so I'm definitely not a candidate for father of the year! If I need to surround myself with children and feel like I have this big extended family, I can always call Brad and Angie and ask them to stay with me, just to remind me why I'm so happy without."

Booyah! Not only does George not have kids—he wants to gently remind you that he's friends with Brad and Angie and lives in a villa in Italy. Try to tell me with a straight face that changing diapers is preferable to drinking wine on Lake Como.

So-called journalists constantly ask him, "But, George, don't you want to be a father?" He recently answered no for the millionth time and also said that he has no plans to dye his hair and that he's going to embrace the gray instead. I want to embrace who I am just like Clooney. (Except I'm dyeing my gray hair every six weeks. Fuck that. Women still haven't mastered that "distinguished gray" thing—we end up looking like vegan Wiccans.)

My old friend Tammy shook my bottle of silver-sparkle nail polish and asked, "Big plans this weekend?"

"No, actually. I'm just going to relax." I tried to concentrate on reading a tabloid. I *did* want to find out how Nicole Richie went from party girl to business owner.

Not one to let her clients read anything without interruption,

Tammy said, "Your husband and kids out of town?" I mean, technically, yes, my husband and kids *were* out of town. My husband was in another town called Ex-Husband-Ville and my kids were in a town many galaxies away called "Nonexistent Limbo." I wanted to give Tammy the benefit of the doubt and assume that she didn't remember that I was the woman she once shamed for not having children—but I saw the look in her eye. She was jabbing at me and not just with her sanitized nail clippers. She knew there was no husband or kids because I looked well rested and didn't have food stains on my shirt. My old instinct kicked in and I answered, "Naaaaaww." We made eye contact and in that moment I thought of my inspiration, George Clooney. Just like me, he did the marriage thing and he couldn't commit, and having children just isn't for people like George and me! But I panicked because I am not George Clooney. I am not friends with Brad and Angie, nor do I have a villa or any self-confidence. So . . . I lied.

I beckoned Tammy close with my unmanicured finger. I whispered, "Can you keep a secret?" I motioned to my uterus or where I think my uterus is—I could have been pointing at my kidney—and said, "I'm expecting. But we haven't told anyone yet because it hasn't been twelve weeks. I'm still nervous."

Tammy dragged her nail file across her mouth to give me the "my lips are sealed" promise. She realized that she had crossed a line in making a pregnant woman tell before it was time. She blushed and waved her hands. "Okay, okay. I see. I see. Just a few weeks along. I ask no more."

Tammy then started yammering to her coworkers in the language of her native country, the place where I'd finally be accepted as a woman who was not dishonoring her family. The other manicurists snapped to and sashayed to my side, like a bunch of chorus boys at the sight of Carol Channing.

The women brought me pillows for my back, warm washcloths for my face. The owner, "Trisha," walked over, clutching a bottle of vanilla-scented lotion. She tapped my shoulder. "Up. Up," she ordered. I leaned forward and she started massaging my neck. "For free. For free," she promised. A free neck massage? A pillow for my back? Even with my 20 percent tips I'd never had this type of attention!

I was having fun watching people believe my lie and I started to tell Tammy the details of my pregnancy, which I'd farmed from listening to my friends talk about their experiences. I told her about the morning sickness, which wasn't so much about throwing up but about how inexplicable nausea gripped me every morning, an uncomfortable sensation akin to taking a vitamin on an empty stomach. I told her about how my food cravings were getting weird—not just what I was eating but how I was eating—and that I went to restaurants and stole french fries off total strangers' plates. I told her about how I was so horny from pregnancy hormones that I took paper towels off their cardboard roll and made a DIY dildo. I told her all about how the bliss from being pregnant made me want to keep the good feeling going, so I tried Ecstasy for the first time and felt the baby kick like she was at a rave.

Tammy touched my knee and said, "Sshhh. You rest." She even closed the magazine in my lap and told me to shut my eyes. I felt like a genius. I got the benefits of motherhood—feeling like I fit in with a tribe of women, not feeling judged, actually being told that it's not rude of me to close my eyes and tune out the person rubbing lotion in between my toes—without having to sit there with a human being growing inside of me and pressing on my bladder, causing me to have to cut the pedicure short so I could pee.

When I went to pay for my mani-pedi, Tammy waved me off. "This one on us." It was like an impromptu surprise baby shower. A free mani-pedi? That's like someone handing me a free thirty-five bucks, which equals two boxes of diapers or six boxes of baby wipes!

While pretending to be pregnant really suited me for a blissful hour of pampering, I resented that I was treated better just because I was a mother-to-be. If I'd shown up at the salon telling everyone about how I'd just worked for ten hours and spent an hour each way in traffic, would I have received a free vanilla-scented neck massage? When I think about Tammy and other women who think like her, I get as angry as I do at homophobes who for some reason can't stop thinking about two men fucking. Mind your own business! All paying customers on Planet Earth deserve a comfortable stay—not just mothers. Even though womanhood technically begins when you get your period, it seems that in our society nobody considers you a woman until you stop getting your period for nine months at a time. Okay. I will admit—that is one huge selling point for pregnancy.

The ladies gave me a curious look when I left, because even though I was only a few weeks pregnant, I stood up and cradled my lower back with my hand, pushing my stomach out as if I were about to give birth. I let out a sigh and waddled toward the front door. I realized I'd forgotten what month into my pregnancy I was and I was behaving as if my water were about to break. But Tammy and Trisha and my new extended family thought I was just a hilarious knocked-up Charlie Chaplin with my physical pregnancy comedy. They clapped and giggled like toddlers watching a thrilling game of peekaboo.

Being fake-pregnant for an afternoon gave me a new perspective on life. I realized, finally, what was important: well, I realized what wasn't important. It is not important to get the approval of people whom I don't know about a very personal decision. As I walked out the door, Tammy threw the bottle of glittery silver nail polish in my purse. She winked at me and said, "Keep it." I accepted her generous gift because with my husband and children permanently out of town and because George Clooney still hadn't invited me to Lake Como, I definitely needed a little sparkle in my weekend.

9. "But You'd Be Such a Good Mom!"

There are a lot of things I might be good at, such as competitive figure skating, window washing from ten stories up, and being an open-heart surgeon. I might also make an excellent kamikaze pilot—except for the fact that I don't want to learn how to fly and have no interest in taking my own life on behalf of Japan.

Recently I ran into my old friend Rich in line at Target. I was standing there with my industrial-size bags of Skittles and a magazine about doing yoga and eating healthy. I was catching him up on the last year of my life, which went something like: "So, yeah, I'm divorced and dating around and I love living alone and I'm working all the time—traveling about every other weekend as well as finishing up my book about being childfree." For some reason, this prompted him to say, "Aw, come on, Jen Kirkman. You'd be such a good mom!"

This statement is at best condescending and at worst patently false and potentially dangerous. It's like telling a friend who you know has a paralyzing fear of wild animals that she would make a great game warden. Seriously, she should just shake off her deep-seated anxiety about being around rhinos and lions and just go out there and guide some poor, innocent family on a safari. I'm sure you'll do fine!

A few years ago, Matt's parents threw us an engagement party at their house. My former future mother-in-law and I stood side by side in the kitchen, prepping for the guests. (Well, I think I was just pouring myself some wine while I awkwardly watched her chop vegetables.) It was an idyllic scene, the two most important women in one man's life, coming together over food and wine. (Okay, I was the only one with the wine.) Sort of semicasually, her knife hand holding the neck of a celery stalk hostage, she said to me, "So, I think we should talk about how you and Matt don't plan to have children."

I braced myself, expecting she'd take a blender, turn it on, and hold my hand over it, threatening, "Tell me again. Tell me one more time that you're not giving me grandchildren. I dare you." I figured she'd at the very least say something like, "You're a horrible, soulless, morally barren woman who is stealing a future family from me and my son!"

Instead, she said very simply, "I support that decision. I participated in the women's movement so that women could have more choices in life and this is one of those choices." I felt relieved. She worked full-time and raised two kids but she didn't try to make me feel like I needed to do the same.

But what would a conversation with your mother-in-law be without a little nugget of guilt that she gets to leave on your pillow before she turns down your metaphorical marital bed?

"Still, I can't say that it isn't a little bit sad to think that I'll never see your children," she continued. "And I know that you two would make great parents if that's what you wanted."

I THINK THAT people confuse a woman with empathy with someone who has the emotional means to raise a child. I'm not mother material but I'm a nice person, sure. And I'm a nice person because I'm usually in a good mood and I'm usually in a good mood because I'm not responsible for raising a child I don't want.

There was this one time, back in 2002, where for a month I helped raise an eight-year-old boy—by accident, after he had an accident in his pants.

"Skyler defecated in his pants in the middle of class and he needs to be picked up from school, immediately." That's what the principal said to me over the phone as I was busy typing up invoices for my boss Jared's flailing set design business that he ran out of his Glendale, California, home. Jared was home but he was locked in his bedroom downstairs, sleeping off a three-bottle wine bender. Skyler wasn't Jared's son. Skyler was Jared's girlfriend's son. Bethany, the girlfriend, wasn't home. She was twenty miles away in Brentwood, taking a yoga class that, as she once bragged, "lots of celebrities and celebrity assistants attend." Bethany was a former catalog model in the Midwest and moved to Los Angeles (well, Glendale) to pursue her dream of . . . some sort of ambiguous fame. She thought that once she was discovered, someone would figure out what to do with her now thirty-seven-year-old body. She would have been the cover model if there were a Los Angeles–based catalog called "Negligent Mothers with Delusions About Their Modeling Careers."

Nobody wants to deal with an eight-year-old boy who pooped himself—especially the administrative assistant to the guy who lives with this kid's biological mother. Although I was self-conscious about driving my two-door Hyundai, which made me feel like I was behind the wheel of an oversize plastic toy car, I still had some pride. It was *my* low-status, oversize plastic toy car and I didn't want someone with shitty-pants to sit in my passenger seat.

The principal said that I wouldn't be allowed to pick up Skyler because I wasn't a relative. I phoned Bethany on her cell and told her that the next pose she needed to get into was "downward driving home" to pick up her son in his shit-stained Spider-Man Underoos. Bethany sighed and said that it would be rude to leave in the middle of class (as opposed to talking on a cell phone in the middle of class?) and that she wouldn't be able to pick up Skyler. She whispered, "Listen, do you know the actor David Duchovny? Well, his personal psychic is here and we're getting along really well. She says that things aren't so good between him and Téa Leoni right now and that it might be the perfect time to introduce me to him. I mean, nothing romantic, but he could keep me in mind for any acting roles. I really shouldn't leave class. I want to talk to her more after." I tried to comprehend that David Duchovny had a psychic and that Bethany thought that she and her crystal ball would be good show business consultants.

Bethany had to call the principal and get me special permission to pick up her son, because the school had this pesky rule about strangers just showing up and grabbing other people's children, putting them in their reasonably priced cars, and driving away.

Before I left to pick up Skyler, I had a momentary maternal (or simply logical) instinct. I brought a few pairs of underwear and a few pairs of his pants. I figured that if I brought him a bunch of clothes, he might feel like he had some control over the situation—it's a task for him to do, pick out his own outfit like a big boy (and hopefully not lose control of his bowels in said outfit this time).

When I got to the school the mother of the other boy involved in the incident started yelling at me. First of all, I didn't know there had been an "incident" and that there was an "other boy"—I thought this was a private matter of Skyler taking a dump in front of the entire classroom. I tried to calm this mother down and explain to her that she should not yell at me, because I'm not Skyler's mother. This enraged her even more. "No wonder he's starting fistfights! Then he shits his pants when my son fought back? He has no mother to teach him manners and no real father to teach him to defend himself. And then they send a secretary to pick up their son?"

I wanted to say, "I'm technically an administrative assistant/bookkeeper. Actually, what I really am is a stand-up comic but things are going a little slow right now." But it didn't seem like a good time to be defensive about my career. This woman had long acrylic nails and a crazed look in her eye that said, "Come at me, girl. I don't care if these zebra-striped babies break on your cute little God-given nose."

Skyler was hiding in the nurses' bathroom because he didn't want me to see him without his pants on. Trust me, I had no interest either. I handed him his clothes through the door—and he said, "Yes! These are my favorites and I'm not allowed to wear these pants to school!" Score one for me. Thank God the school nurse had already cleaned Skyler's underwear and hosed him down or whatever you do when a kid does a number two in an unauthorized area. I took his hand as he left the bathroom, and as the other boy's mother yelled, "Coward!" in Skyler's face, I felt a wave of rage. I wanted justice. I put my finger to her lips and I said, "You *do not* speak to a child like that. He will be disciplined but *not* by you. Do you hear me?" And with that, I grabbed my son-for-a-day's hand and we left. I felt like the mom from *Good Times*.

Just like I had done so many times in my own life, Skyler got into my car and immediately started crying. He sobbed, "Everyone is making fun of me for pooping at school." I thought about my experience as a stand-up comedian and how when I get heckled I think, *At least I get to stand here for a living, making money right now, and you people have to look at me. I'm the one who's doing a fun thing no matter how much you think I suck.* So I said to him, "It is pretty gross that you pooped yourself. Right? If it wasn't gross, you wouldn't have changed your pants!" He started to giggle. I figured I was onto something so I went on: "But it's normal. You got scared. And you know what? *You* got to leave school early. All those kids who are making fun of you—still have to be at school for three more hours! So if they make fun of you tomorrow, maybe you can make a joke."

"Yeah!" he said. "I'll tell them that if they were smart, they would poop and get to leave school early. I'm a genius!"

I laughed. I have no idea if this was an appropriate way to handle the situation but at least I was there. His mother was doing a sun salutation and plotting to steal Téa Leoni's husband.

Honestly I never liked Skyler that much. He was fresh. He would tip over my pen cup every day at my desk, which was in the living room. Since his mother never disciplined him, he would watch cartoons turned up really loud while I was trying to work. One time when I was feeling really badly and desperately trying to find another job by searching online job listings on my current employer's computer, Skyler turned on a TV program superloud. He said, "Jen, do you think this guy is funny?" I turned around and was face-to-TV with Blake, my tuna-fish-stealing, feathered-hair-sporting ex-boyfriend from college. He was the host of a hugely popular children's show on Nickelodeon. This show had been on TV for years, whereas the last show I had appeared on was GSN's *Funny Money*—a now defunct game show where comedians did snippets of their acts in order to help contestants win money. The contestant I was paired up with lost all of her money and I bombed with a terrible "at least getting dumped is better than having cancer" joke.

"What's wrong?" Skyler asked.

I wanted to stay strong in front of an eight-year-old but I started to cry a little bit. "I know him," I said.

"Is he your boyfriend?"

"Not anymore."

"How come he doesn't love you anymore?" Skyler asked. "Is it because he's on TV?"

Now I wanted to punch this kid but I also wanted to sit on the couch next to him and say, "Skyler, you're never going to forget your first real love. You think you're doing fine and you haven't seen him in years and then he's on TV pouring syrup on his cohost's head and you think . . . maybe if I'd stayed with him, my life could look the way I want it to look." But I said none of that. Because the next thing out of Skyler's mouth was, "I think you are a nicer person than him and I like you. So don't be sad."

How did this kid who had no parental guidance find it in his heart to want to help take care of me—a stupid administrative assistant who picked him up once after he shit his pants?

Does that one selfless act on my part (which was also technically my job) prove that I would be such a good mom? I don't think so. I think I'd be so overwhelmed and unhappy about raising a child that

I would turn into the asshole in yoga class trying to put my leg over my head and hoping to run into David Duchovny's psychic.

TWO YEARS AGO when our best friends, Grace and Christopher, called us to change the location of our standing Saturday-night double date, I was instantly suspicious. Instead of making a reservation at a restaurant, they wanted us to come to their house to avoid "noise" and "crowds." We're not that cool. We never went anywhere hip, noisy, or crowded.

When Grace and Christopher bought their house a few years ago, the first thing they pointed out to us was their guest bedroom. "If you guys get wasted, you don't have to drive home!" On this night, Matt and I walked into their house and they sat us right down at the dining room table. We skipped our usual predinner cocktails, and I noticed only *one* bottle of wine was on the table. I eyed their sidebar—no bottles sat waiting to be opened. Grace was drinking water and pretending to be totally into it even though we spent countless Saturday nights in the past getting near-hiccups from drinking Viognier and crying, "No, *you're* my good friend." "No, *you* are."

I wanted to say, "Grace, you're obviously pregnant and you have to wait the doctor-advised twelve weeks to tell people, but you can tell me. I promise I won't blog about it," but even I understand there are boundaries here. When my dear childhood friend Shannon was first pregnant, I happened to be visiting her in our hometown in Massachusetts. She pulled the classic lie that every pregnant woman tells: "I'm not going to have a cocktail with dinner because I'm on antibiotics. I have a cold." You have a cold? Really? Why aren't you sneezing? Why didn't you cancel our date to go out for drinks if you had a cold? Why did you go to work today? No woman I know would ever listen to her doctor's warnings about alcohol—unless she was pregnant. If a doctor said to any of my girlfriends, "Even one glass of wine tonight could bring about Armageddon," they'd be like, "Well, we've had fun here while it lasted. Can I get a pinot grigio?"

Grace and Christopher made their big announcement. After years of being on the fence, they were going to have a baby. My heart sang for them and then sank for me. I was scared. I'm the baby of the family so I never experienced the terror of my parents saying, "You're going to have a little sister," and me whining, "But I like how things are! I don't want to make room for any new people!"

Everything was going to change. Even though we'd never actually been wasted enough to have to spend the night in their guest room, I liked that it was there. It represented a spontaneity that I could . . . count on. Now the only drooling and helpless creature in the Drunken Guest Room would be a baby. And what about my hikes with Grace? Would I still be able to run off into the woods with my pregnant friend and talk about my secret younger-man-in-a-band sex fantasies or would I be too self-conscious around the baby's undeveloped earbuds to say anything dirty? Would we have to cancel our weekend lunch because Lamaze class ran long? Are Lamaze classes even still a thing?

As Grace and Christopher told us the story of what the last eight weeks of pregnancy had been like, I remembered a conversation I'd had with Grace recently. I realized now that she'd been trying to tell me that she'd changed her mind about having kids a few weeks earlier when she asked, "Did you see the YouTube video of that chimpanzee that just gave birth?"

"No. Gross. I'm sorry you had to see that," I answered.

"No, Jen. The mother and baby were bonding. She just instinctively licked her wounds and tended to her baby. It was so natural."

"Well, of course it's natural. All monkeys do is fuck and have babies, right?"

"It got me thinking, even though I'm worried about bringing a child into the world, I'm still an animal with normal urges and I can't intellectualize that sense of hope I feel."

I completely missed out on what she was probably trying to tell me and dismissed her with, "Well, thank God we're not monkeys!

We can take birth control! Speaking of primal urges, have you ever fantasized about having sex with a twentysomething painter?"

On the drive home (we didn't get drunk enough to warrant that spare room sleepover) I said to Matt, "Once that baby is born we are never going to see them again." I knew what was coming—this wasn't my first baby rodeo. (Sidebar: Even I can admit that a baby rodeo would be very cute—although stressful. You don't want to fall off a horse when you still have that soft spot on your skull.) As usual, Matt thought I was being dramatic (I was). He explained to me that when two people love each other very much and want to make a baby—they can still hang out with their friends just like always, except there will be a baby in the room. I explained to *him* that everybody knows your dumb friends coming over to order Chinese food can interrupt the bonding process between mother and father and child. Even doctors say you need at least three months of constant bonding to make a healthy relationship with your baby. But I am like a baby, and if I lose three months of bonding with my girlfriends, my development is affected and I start peeing myself just to get some goddamned attention.

Nobody gets babysitters anymore, do they? That's so eighties. If we want to see our friends, we'll have to go to their house all the time and have whisper-around-the-table-because-the-baby-is-sleeping early dinners. I feared that Grace and Christopher would turn into the type of parents I'd lost touch with because their kids became their entire life:

"So . . . seen any good movies lately?"

"We don't have time to go to movies anymore."

"Oh, that's right. We forgot. So . . . seen any good TV shows lately?"

"No. We don't want to zone out on our kid—so as a family the only entertainment we partake in is playing with organic wooden blocks."

"So . . . read any interesting newspaper articles lately?"

"No. With the baby, I don't even have time to shower, so I just rub a newspaper all over my body to soak up the oil and sweat. After that it's unreadable and I'm covered in ink."

Then there's always that awkward silence and your girlfriend will ask, "So . . . how's your mom? Didn't you say she was going to get a suspicious mole checked out?"

"Oh, yes. Actually we had a little bit of a scare. My mom got her test results back and they were—" The baby cries.

"Oh, I'm sorry," she'll say, "I can't go and pick up the baby because he has to learn how to just cry, but I want to stand within twelve feet of him so that he can smell my pheromones and moisturizer. Hold that thought. I'll be right back."

The baby is eventually lulled back to sleep and Mom comes back only to *not* pick up where she left off, because the 7:30 p.m. yawning has commenced. She'll never hear what I was going to say about my mom's melanoma because she's desperate for everyone to leave so she and her husband can sleep for two hours before their baby wakes up to practice crying and going to sleep without being picked up.

"Jen," Matt said. "Your mom doesn't have cancer and Grace and Christopher's baby hasn't even been born."

"I know that! But I'm saying if she did—our friends with kids would not have time to console me. This is a real concern, Matt. We have to brace ourselves in the event that we lose Grace and Christopher to the other side."

I envisioned the next phase of losing my friends to their children, which is when the people with kids realize that their childfree friends don't have any handy tips for them based on their own experience. I have no idea whether they should switch from breast milk to formula after a month or whether organic cotton is better on their baby's bottom than recycled hemp cotton. So parents naturally gravitate toward other parents and they start to speak their own language. Nobody needs a childfree person there—it wastes too much time to try to translate.

I'm just going to come out and say it: this is the real reason lots of people end up changing their minds and having kids. They don't want to lose their friends. It's just like drugs. Peer pressure eventually gets to everyone. No one wants to be the narc or someone who is harshing everyone's illegal substance– or pregnancy hormone–induced good vibe. This is exactly what happened to Keith Richards.

Have I mentioned I am the baby of the family? Still, whenever someone asks me why I don't want to have kids, I think about how abandoned I feel when my friends get pregnant and that's usually the last little tiny little hint of a feeling that pushes me into the maybe territory—I just want my life to stay the same and keep my friends. Then I remember that losing sleep, picking boogers out of a child's nose, and having said booger maker wake me up every day at five thirty is not worth my bringing a human life into the world just because I could *probably* mimic the other parent chimps in the wild and manage to raise a kid without killing it. (Do chimps sometimes eat their kids? I should look that up but I'm too lazy. I wouldn't even be a good researcher, let alone mom. I'm just not curious enough.)

People say this to me a lot, that I would be such a good mom. I'm not even that good of an aunt. Ask my nieces and nephews. I missed both of their high school graduations and one college graduation because I was stuck in a casino for the weekend. Fine, I wasn't on a wine spritzer and bingo bender—I was doing stand-up comedy for tables of bachelorette parties with penis hats on their heads.

In fact, if I'm being honest, the person who drove the biggest wedge between Shannon and Tracy and me—was *me*. I moved thousands of miles away from Massachusetts to California. If I lived on the East Coast, I would see my childhood friends all of the time; we'd call bomb threats in to one another's places of business just so that we could take long lunches together, we'd use our health insurance and check into an inpatient "exhaustion rehab center" for a week as a way to get a free spa experience, and we'd go walk around all of the many prestigious Boston college and university campuses just to see whether we look young enough to get hit on. But they've moved on to the next phase in their lives and I have in mine—although I never would have predicted that my next phase would involve my marriage ending, not my friendships.

My fears about Grace and Christopher were completely unfounded. They didn't change once they had their baby. They have a babysitter. We hang out. And I'm the one who whispers around the dinner table when they've never asked me to. I just didn't feel comfortable saying things like, "We were sleeping together, it was never serious. He has kind of a crooked penis, which is no problem but I think it makes him self-conscious," at normal volume in front of their infant—I don't know what kids these days pick up on!

When I see Shannon with her sons I feel like I'm watching her star in a play called *The Good Mom*. The play opened Off Broadway and people didn't notice it at first, but the reviews were so good once the critics realized that they had a capable and competent ingenue who could deliver a tour-de-force performance without seeming tired and without one beautiful blond hair falling out of place. She's a parent and it makes her really happy. And just like somebody's mother would, I still see her as a little girl. And because she and Tracy are my little girls—I absolutely love their children. I want to take their toddlers aside and tell them stories about all of the bad poetry Shannon wrote and how when you are fresh to your aunt Tracy it breaks my heart because she's supercool—she holds the high score among our friends in Super Mario Bros. and she used to dye her hair purple.

I know I wouldn't be a good mom but I'm a pretty good gift-buyer for my mommy friends. I bought Richard Scarry's *Best Storybook Ever* for Shannon's son Ben, and years later he still asks her to read it to him every night. Every freaking night! I always hated reading to kids because you're never *really* reading. They're so young and don't have a grasp of the English language yet; they just want you to point at the pictures and they completely ignore the narrative, and when you're getting to the good part they grab the corner of the book and try to put it in their mouth. If I had a kid of my own, I'd be pissed. *Hey, what makes you think you should put this in your mouth?*

It's not on a plate hot out of the oven. This is a book. B-o-o-k, *not* food. F-o-o-d. *God. Is my kid going to be a nincompoop? He is eating a book instead of reading it. I think I need to return him. I hope he's covered under the manufacturer's warranty.*

When I was interviewing Grace for this book, her sixteen-month-old daughter, Delia, fell face-first on the porch right in front of me as I was taking a bite of my sandwich. I threw the sandwich down, spit up my bites, and screamed. "Ohmygod! Ohmygod! Grace!! Grace!! *She fell!*" My instinct was to flee like I do in other uncomfortable backyard situations, involving wasps and small talk with neighbors who pop in unexpectedly. Delia just looked at me, utterly confused. Her lip curled like Elvis's and she seemed to be thinking, *Uh-oh. I'm not equipped to deal with this woman's impending breakdown.* Then she got back up like nothing happened and continued pushing her little cart filled with her favorite things: a doll, a purse, some blocks, and a napkin.

Grace explained that unlike our parents—Mommy kissed your boo-boo only after she said, "Oh, Jesus Christ, you made me spill my drink," or she panicked, cried, and wondered out loud in front of you whether she needed to call 911 and whether you would die in your sleep during naptime after what was obviously a concussion—today's parents don't show their hand. Today's parents don't react emotionally in front of their kids. It scares the kid to hear you scream, "Oh my God—I wanted you to live to see your second birthday!" And it hurts your kids' feelings to act like you are inconvenienced by the fact that they are just learning how to balance on their own two feet in this world filled with gravity. It's genius, really. I would try it if I ever wanted to be a good mom, which I don't.

Grace also told me she was learning that kids are scientists—not assholes who are trying to fuck with you. So when they do try to eat dirt for the second time, after you told them the first time that it's not the best idea, don't take it personally and tell them how stupid they are. Simply see them as scientists who need to keep testing their dirt-eating hypothesis over and over. (I don't know whether this theory also comes in handy later, when a teenage girl keeps dating alcoholics. I know that if I were a parent, I wouldn't want to watch Billy tear through the driveway with a six-pack in his Camaro and tell myself that my teenage daughter is just being a scientist and that this ingrate Billy is her "lab partner.")

Every second spent with Grace's kid warms my heart. She and Christopher made a person and they are in love with this little person. And I'm in love with love when I'm around them. And then when I get home and lie on the couch I am so happy that there aren't any little scientists of my own running around and falling down and courting concussions and bad-news boyfriends.

Grace once described loving Delia like this: "I feel like when I see her walking around, that my heart has been removed from my chest and it's just running around on a stick." That's actually beautiful if you think about it and I get what she means. I just have no interest in my heart being on a stick. It could be the fact that I'm a vegetarian. I've never been a fan of satay.

WHEN WE WERE married, Matt and I often told people that we were a family, just the two of us. That sentiment felt secure and it was true. We were legally a family. But people who had kids usually just looked at us with pity—the kind of pity I reserve for people who are folding and unfolding strollers and clumsily walking into a restaurant.

I knew that people stared at us and thought, *But you can't have a two-person family. What if one of you falls off a boat when you're on vacation? Then what? A family of one? What good is a family of one? If you're the only one in your family, then who do you blame for all of your mistakes? No, it's your fault that I dropped the carton of orange juice that I was drinking from while standing in front of the open refrigerator, because you walked into the kitchen on your tiptoes. You know that when you try to walk quietly it scares me more than if you just walked normally. Also, I had a bad day at work and I blame you because if it weren't for you,*

I'd have more free time to meet the heir to an oil empire and if he married me—I'd never have to work again! I'm not feeling good about myself but I'm too afraid to look within, so I'm just going to fixate on the fact that your toothbrush is on the top of our toilet tank.

I imagine that if Matt had come home every night and said to me, "Oh, Jen, but you'd be such a good cook," our marriage would have broken up a lot faster than it did.

It's not that I can't cook. I just don't enjoy cooking. It takes too long and you have to stand there monitoring everything, which doesn't work well for me and my ADHD. The times that I've cooked something elaborate in my kitchen, I've packed for the event like I'm going on a long plane ride. I make sure I have my laptop, BlackBerry, iPod, a book, and some magazines at arm's length.

Throughout most of my life there seemed to be only two types of women represented on TV shows. There were housewives slaving away over a hot stove and then there was *Sex and the City*'s Carrie Bradshaw, who once said she used her stove to store handbags. I'm neither of these types of woman. Before and after we were married, my husband's dinner would continue to be something that he bought for himself at the Whole Foods sandwich counter. I'd be coming home from work at nine o'clock and eating my cottage-cheese-and-cucumber saltine sandwiches. I wasn't a totally useless wife. I was always able to open a bottle of wine for dessert.

I have memories of my grandfather Kirkman making mashed potatoes that were so good because they tasted like a bowl of butter. I love my mom's brownies. My favorite thing about both of those recipes is that someone else made them for me. Occasionally I feel an urge to whip up some mashed potatoes and brownies, but I don't ever feel an urge to scrape the crust from the baking pan, or to squeeze out some progeny so he or she can remember that while Mommy was out of town often doing stand-up comedy, she baked a mean banana bread to try to make up for her flagrant neglect.

I am a generally honest, good person who likes eating your brownies/playing with your kid for ten minutes, but that doesn't mean I should drop everything and enroll in culinary school or start begetting future generations so that one day I can traumatize them, for example by telling them their grandpa was a no-good adulterer.

I never met my mom's dad, Grandpa Freddy, who died many years before I was born. I'd always known my (now deceased) Nana Jean as a widow. Nana lived about an hour away from our house and had never learned to drive. Once a year, on Thanksgiving, my dad dutifully picked up his mother-in-law and drove her back to Needham, Massachusetts, to stay with us. Nana and I used to walk to the corner doughnut shop the morning of her arrival and when we were out of earshot of my mom, she'd tell me stories about her dead husband. That's how I thought of Grandpa Freddy—as my nana's dead husband and not a real grandfatherly type. She didn't paint the most familial picture of that man.

Apparently, Freddy was a bit of a womanizer and cheated on my nana. When I was about nine, on one of our doughnut-eating walks, I asked her, "Is Grandpa in hell?" I knew the Catholic Church wasn't so hot on married men having girlfriends, and even though he was my grandfather, I was pretty sure that God didn't bend the rules for my family. Nana matter-of-factly answered, "Freddy's in purgatory."

She explained that it was like a waiting-room area for people who are dead but aren't quite ready to meet God. That didn't sound so bad. I liked most waiting rooms as long as they had fish tanks and *Highlights* magazine. But Nana Jean said that purgatory was brutal. She said it felt like you just couldn't wait anymore and then the nurse would come out and you would see a glimpse of God behind her and she'd look you over and decide not to take you in to see him just yet. All the while the devil is nipping at your heels, saying, "I'll take you right now if you want." My nana grinned. "I know Freddy's in purgatory because his spirit knocks on the wall above my bed all night long while I'm sleeping. And I say, 'Freddy, since when do you pay so much attention to me in the bedroom?' Freddy wants me to pray for him. That's how he'll get out of purgatory. But I'm not praying for him. He can wait."

I never had to go to Catholic school like my mom did. My parents weren't as religious as their parents. My parents were like middle managers to God the CEO. They passed on his orders with a shrug: "Look, I don't want to strictly obey the Ten Commandments either but the big guy says we have to."

But straying from Catholicism makes my mom nervous because her superstition kicks in. I'll never forget when I told her that I'd started going to Buddhist lectures in Los Angeles. "Jennifah, you can't do that. You were baptized in the Catholic Church. There's an invisible mark on you that says, 'Catholic.' You can't go get stamped with other religions. God doesn't know what to make of it and you don't end up in heaven."

For such an all-powerful dude, God, as my mom sees him, is easily confused. I did have to go to church every Sunday, although we didn't pray or read the Bible at home during the week or anything like that. My mom's philosophy was: "God is busy. He doesn't need to hear that you're thankful for every shit and fart." I always thought that expression should be embroidered on a pillow.

Ultimately I decided Buddhism wasn't for me either. You still have to get up on Sunday mornings and you have to sit twice as still for twice as long. My mom also has given up going to church. She thinks the pastors are too old and out of touch. She and my dad have found the church of Foxwoods Casino in Connecticut, where they are devoted to the worship of the slot machines. Another of my mom's philosophies is: "Well, at least the church I'm *not* going to is the *right* one."

But like all good Catholic families, ours just keeps getting bigger. I've come to realize that my relatives apparently like to have lots of unprotected sex. The annual Kirkman Christmas party is getting so enormous and overwhelming that I've had to start my own tradition for that day—have a phone-therapy session with my shrink in the morning while trying to mask the fact that I'm sipping a 10:00 a.m. glass of Riesling.

Every party is the same. I say about two sentences to a cousin and then their daughter, whatsherface, is off and running across the room to put her finger in a light socket to see whether she'll light up like the Christmas tree. The fact that I don't want to have kids of my own doesn't mean I want to watch someone else's die a painful death by electrocution, so I gracefully bow out of the conversation. "No, it's fine. You go chase her. We'll catch up later."

My extended family are a bunch of hospitable, sweet souls. Anyone who walks through the door is considered family. But sometimes I'm still self-conscious at the family Christmas party because I am childless. My sister Violet is childless too but she has three cats and three horses. She gets up at the crack of dawn to feed them, so people feel less bad for her. It seems like as long as you're cleaning up some living thing's poop after age thirty, family members really respect that lifestyle choice. My uncle Will, a stout Italian man with a white beard, plays Santa Claus every year at the party. Kirkman Christmas takes place a week before Actual Christmas, but the kids are naturally able to suspend their disbelief and accept that Santa Claus comes to Auntie Violet's a week early to honor the fact that it's easier to get all of the Kirkmans together on that day. Also, when you're a kid, I guess it's just called "believing in Santa" and not "suspension of disbelief."

At dusk, Uncle Will heads out to my sister's barn and changes into his red Santa suit, complete with fake white beard, even though he has a real one underneath. He brings in a sackful of presents and doles them out to more than thirty screaming, shrieking children who are freaking out harder than preteen girls and creepy older men at a Justin Bieber concert.

I stand back with the adults while the kids trample one another for a front-row seat at the Santa concert, and once they're down, I watch them go into a trance. At no point do they seem to realize that Santa, unlike any other man, has whiskers made of cotton. Or maybe they do notice but don't seem to care? I never thought that any of the Santas I met as a kid was *the* Santa.

My mom always told me that the Santa Claus at the mall was a

Santa look-alike who was also from the North Pole and definitely sanctioned by Santa. So I never went in with expectations and I always felt a little superior to the other kids because I knew that this wasn't Santa and I was in on it with him. I'd sit on his lap and play the game and tell him what I wanted, knowing that he would pass it on to the real Santa but that the chump whose lap I was sitting on was not the guy who was going to be coming down our chimney.

Actually, nobody was coming down our chimney. We didn't have a fireplace. My mom told me that Santa came in through a vent on the roof and climbed down our attic stairs (which doubled as a cleaning supplies closet). I was always very impressed with how, every Christmas morning, the cleaning supplies looked untouched. Santa got extra points in my book for being so diligent about putting things back where they belonged.

But every kid at Kirkman Christmas was told that this was *the* Santa Claus. And they were buying the taped-on eyebrows that Uncle Will was selling.

By the time Will/Santa comes on the scene, the shrieking gets out of control. I don't remember my mother and father ever letting me shriek at high decibels in other people's homes—even family members' homes. I've never grabbed someone's Christmas gift out of his or her hands. (Then again, I never wanted the same kind of presents that other kids got. As a kid, every Christmas I asked Santa Claus for one of those "furry clips that high school girls hang off their purses." Santa never delivered. I learned later in life that those are known as "roach clips" and they are not just purse decorations, like some pinecone ornament on a Christmas tree. They hold your roach—aka the tiny little pile of ash and rolling papers that a joint has been reduced to after a round of puffing and passing.)

At last year's Kirkman Christmas party, with my divorce still a secret and it being no secret that I was beyond my peak egg health, I thought it would be a good strategy to seem "normal" and "into children." When Santa had given out his last gift and the kids' voices were hoarse from wailing, I decided to flex my maternal side.

Everybody was always telling me I'd be such a great mom and the third glass of Riesling had given me the courage to try. Santa Will walked quickly toward the front door with his empty bag. Once he was out of their eye line, the kids had already forgotten about Santa. They were playing with their toys and almost knocking over the Christmas tree. The front door shut and I ran to the group of kids and said, "You guys! Santa is leaving! Let's all run to the window and watch his sleigh with his reindeers fly away!" The kids looked at me in stunned silence. *They had never considered that the sleigh and eight tiny reindeer were outside.* I was a genius. Here I had been for thirty-seven years, thinking that I wasn't good with kids just because I didn't want a child of my own, and it turns out I possessed, at minimum, the creativity of a cool kindergarten teacher.

The kids screamed in unison, *"Rudolph!"* and ran to the window. They pushed one another from side to side, trying to get the best view, just as I realized that the view they were getting was a behind-the-curtain glimpse of Uncle Will going to his truck to drop off his empty bag and walking into the barn to change back into his plain red fleece KISS THE COOK sweatshirt—an outfit not becoming of Rachael Ray, let alone a magic man like Santa.

Some kids saw Santa Will walk into the barn and the kids who didn't were crying because they'd missed the sleigh flying away. The rest of them couldn't figure out what the hell was going on, so they just started to cry in utter confusion. It was like watching a bunch of women having dinner together and one of them starts to get choked up. But before she has a chance to explain why she's about to start sobbing the others join in—partly due to an instinct to sympathize and partly due to the competitive instinct to steal the sympathy spotlight. *I am the most upset! Look at me!*

My aunt Gina turned to me and said, "Here's a tip. When dealing with children, you don't have to act like a child. You just have to tell them to believe in Santa Claus but don't exhaust yourself running around acting like you believe in him too."

Maybe that's a good reason to tell people why I'm not having kids. Part of being a good mom is suspension of disbelief, trusting your kids will grow up to be awesome instead of jobless burnouts, trusting that they won't get bullied or that at least you'll know what to do if they do, trusting you won't lose all of your friends and you'll get your boobs back. I'm not really equipped to tell someone to believe in something that I can't believe in too. And I don't want to raise someone so blindly trusting of me that he or she actually thinks a fat guy who probably can't catch his own breath has the energy to oversee an entire workforce of elves three hundred and sixty-five days a year, and that somehow with no workouts or training he can keep his arms flapping on those reins all night long on a sleigh that holds enough toys for all of the children in the world—except for the Jewish and Muslim kids.

If I had a kid, I already know that I would totally break her trust later in life when I go into her room and read her diary. That's why I'm folding now.

10. I'm Gonna Die Alone (and I Feel Fine)

Mrs. Sanders, the ninety-two-year-old lady who lived across the street from me when I was a little kid, died alone trying to change a bulb in the Tiffany light fixture on her kitchen ceiling. In what should be documented as the biggest "are you fucking kidding me" in the history of bad timing, she had a heart attack while standing on the chair and fell backward, and only the kitchen floor was there to break her fall and her brittle bones. She was found on her back, clutching a sixty-watt bulb, next to a tipped-over chair, while her apparently necrophiliac poodle, Mimi, licked her face. She had a "kid"—a seventy-two-year-old son named Donny who didn't live with her. He wasn't there to take charge and say, "Mom, I'll change the lightbulb for you. Please, don't climb that chair. You could fall to your death on the floor, where I will find you in a day with your housedress over your head and your knee-high panty hose exposed."

I think of Mrs. Sanders whenever somebody says to me, "If you don't have kids, you won't have anyone to take care of you when you're old." Mrs. Sanders sacrificed her best years in metabolism— her twenties and thirties—to raise Donny, and she still ended up changing her own lightbulb, which led to her taking her last breath alone in the dark on some cold linoleum. Donny came by every week to help his mom grocery shop and to weed her flower garden, but he wasn't there on the night that he could have been most helpful. According to the logic of bearing children in order to have built-in caretaker insurance, if Mrs. Sanders birthed Donny only so she could get some help around the house in her twilight years, she wasted her life.

Obviously I realize that having a kid who doesn't end up changing your lightbulb one time and therefore not preventing your untimely death doesn't *necessarily* mean your life was wasted. But she could have just skipped the whole "raising Donny" thing and been a swinging-single flapper, swilling gin at speakeasies. Sure, she still might have died on the kitchen floor, but it could have been because she was being taken by a handsome gentleman with a jaunty fedora and due to the strong gin, she tilted backward in ecstasy, hitting her head and falling to her death on the floor in the throes of passion— her last words of "Oh, God!" left up to interpretation.

WE ALL KNOW we're going to die, right? That's why a lot of us either *find* religion or *fear* religion. Knowing we're going to die is why some of us take medication or self-medicate. Knowing that you're going to die might make you indulge in eating comfort foods or want instant gratification or combine the two as you sit in the car and open a pint of Ben & Jerry's you just bought at the grocery store, holding it in front of the dashboard's heat vent until the AmeriCone Dream is no longer totally frozen, and then taking a bite out of the top without a spoon. "Who cares that I'm eating ice cream with my bare hands? I'm going to die alone," you say to yourself as you drive with one hand, holding the pint between your teeth and wiping your sticky fingers on the passenger seat.

Knowing I'm going to die someday has never filled me with the desire to make another human being, whom I have to spend the "good years" of my life looking after in hopes that someday he or she might return the favor. What if you died during childbirth? Then you've screwed yourself out of a life *and* you'll have created a person who will have no elderly mother to take care of someday.

In the song "Beautiful Boy," which he wrote for his son Sean Lennon, John Lennon sang, "Life is what happens to you while you're busy making other plans." And I say, "While you're busy making other plans, hoping that one day your teenagers will grow up to be adults who sponge-bathe you, they're hiding behind the local 7-Eleven doing whip-its."

Have a baby: Just add water and boom! Instant caretaker! Guaranteed to bring you your high blood pressure medication and administer your insulin shots! But what if your kid grows up to be completely inept? These are a handful of possible outcomes for your child's life that could hinder his or her ability to be your emergency contact, let alone care for you in your old age:

- Your daughter is busy trying to make a living as a reality TV star and most of her days are spent in undisclosed locations so that the rose ceremony results remain confidential.
- Your son is a commercial pilot with a drinking problem and bad depth perception who flies exclusively in the Rocky Mountains.
- Your son is a scientist—only because he secretly wants access to Bunsen burners so that he can continue with his after-work meth-making hobby.
- Your daughter is a stand-up comedian.
- Your kid ends up being the teenage boy who waited on me at a Best Buy in Las Vegas. His name tag said BREN—is that a name? Creative naming is a blueprint for making either an angry outcast or an entitled hipster—and both of those types of guys end up being completely unfuckable in their early twenties, wearing their short-sleeved plaid shirts and Malcolm X–style black-rimmed glasses.

Anyway, I'd gone into the Las Vegas Strip–adjacent Best Buy during my friend's destination birthday party weekend, scrambling last minute to buy what would hopefully be the best birthday gift I could give her—the *Golden Girls* DVD boxed set. Young Bren appeared to be sleeping standing up when I approached him at the counter. He literally looked like he had the weight of the world on his shoulders—as if gravity and the mere effort it took to stand up against it were too much for this kid to handle as he worked his Saturday-afternoon shift in the DVD section. Or maybe it was just the weight of those weird plug earrings that were stretching his lobes to the size of a dilated-and-about-to-give-birth vagina.

I wasn't sure how to approach a teenager who was dozed off in the upright position. I knew from dealing with my sister's horse that any sudden touch or loud noise could cause him to buck and kick me under the chin with his dirty Converse low-tops. I kept a safe distance of a few feet and said deliberately, "Excuse me, Bren?" (I tried not to say "Bren" judgmentally.)

He snorted, grunted, grumbled, wiped his nose and eyes, and said, "Oh, uh, yeah? Hey." I felt like I was his mom. *Bren, wake up! It's time for school!* I thought back to when I was a cashier at Roche Bros. grocery store in Needham and how I got in trouble with the store manager after a customer complained that when she approached me, I had my hair in my face as I bundled the one-dollar bills in the cash register. No manager was anywhere in sight at the Best Buy. Bren was a lone scarecrow overseeing the crops of DVDs spread out before us. Our conversation was as follows:

Me: "Hi. I'm looking for a DVD boxed set. Do you have *The Golden Girls*?"
Bren: "You mean *Gilmore Girls*?"
Me: "No. I don't mean *Gilmore Girls*. I mean *The Golden Girls*."
Bren: "Um, wait, do you mean the Golden Globes?"
(Is there even such a thing? Yeah, I want the Golden Globes DVD boxed set. *All of them*—starting with the first Golden Globes ceremony back in 1944. Don't skimp on one part! I want all of it—including every best short black-and-white cartoon that has a hint of racism. I have a U-Haul outside

and a storage space that I'm dying to fill up with over sixty
years of awards shows.)

Me: "No. Not the Golden Globes. Not *Gilmore Girls*. The *Golden
Girls*."

Bren: "Uhhh, what's that?"

Me: "What's *The Golden Girls*?"

Bren: "Yeah. I don't know what that is."

"Bren," I said, "*The Golden Girls*. Starring Bea Arthur, Rue McClana-
han, Betty White, and Estelle Getty. Four middle-age/elderly women
living together. Some were divorced, some widowed—but it didn't
matter, they didn't need men. They had one another. Not to say that
they weren't still sexual—they were. Especially Blanche. *The Golden
Girls!* The original *Sex and the City*, if you will. Saturday nights on
NBC!"

Bren dismissed the entire run of the show with a simple, "Pshhhht.
Oh. I never heard of it."

"But it was one of the most popular sitcoms from the 1980s!"

Bren shook his head. "Well, I don't need to know that. I was born
in the nineties."

Born in the nineties? I can't even imagine such a thing. How can
anyone not have been a teenager in 1991 when Nirvana's teen anthem album *Nevermind* came out? How does being a teenager not
involve driving around in a flannel shirt in your parents' Oldsmobile, listening to the local college station, just waiting for "Smells
Like Teen Spirit" to come on the radio? The nineties were meant for
being a teenager—if they weren't, Nirvana would have named their
hit anthem "Smells Like Just Being Born," and that conjures up the
smell of regurgitated stale oatmeal and sour milk. If Kurt Cobain
were still alive, he'd kill himself all over again because teenagers
these days are so stupid.

I hate the arrogance of "I don't need to know that." I'm sure he
knows the name of every character in *Star Wars*—does he need to
know that? It's certainly not helping him get laid. By the time I was

a toddler in the late 1970s I knew that although James Dean was a teen idol for girls in the 1950s, in his real life he took ballet class and was rumored to be bisexual, or, as my mother would say, "a little bit AC/DC." I knew that Marilyn Monroe had "committed suicide," but lots of people believed her death was a swift assassination by the Kennedys, because after sleeping with Bobby *and* Jack she simply "knew too much" about their mob ties.

If Bren had no idea about things that happened before the nineties, he must watch *American Idol* and think, *This old guy Steven Tyler seems to know what he's talking about. I agree with everything he says even though I have no idea what qualifies this nail polish–wearing man whom I've never heard of to judge a singing competition!* Bren must get blown away walking into an Urban Outfitters and seeing a Rubik's Cube being ironically sold at the counter and thinking, *Hey, look! It's a three-dimensional app! Whoa! How do I get that into my iPhone?*

When people breathlessly and worriedly ask me, "But . . . but if you don't have kids, who will take care of you when you're old?" I think, *Not these dummies!* If I'm in a nursing home, I want someone my own age or close to it administering my meds. I don't want some young Bren type to have my life in his hands as he says, "Uh, you want me to give that old lady some penicillin? What is that—some drug that was discovered in 1928? Shit. I don't need to know about this. I was born in the nineties."

I disagree somewhat with Eckhart Tolle. I'm not sure I like the concept of "the power of now." I want to write a new-age book called *The Power of Nostalgia* geared at teenagers like Bren who think that they don't need to know about anything that came before them. Would he say, "I don't need to know that," in history class when his teacher says that it's time to learn about evil dictators? Let us not forget that those who cannot remember the past are condemned to repeat it. I'm not saying that knowing about the episode of *The Golden Girls* where Blanche's much younger fitness instructor asks her out will inspire genius in today's youth, but maybe Mussolini wouldn't have been such a power-hungry asshole if he'd had more laughs as a young boy.

MY NANA REFUSED to leave her modest five-room ranch-style home in Methuen, Massachusetts, even well into her nineties. She was mowing her own lawn in her eighties and precariously kneeling on her kitchen counter to paint her cabinets to relieve boredom. She walked down flights of stairs while she was dizzy from her high blood pressure medication so that she could get to the laundry room in the basement. My mom and my uncle tried to get her to stop—but short of moving in with Nana and sitting on her, they couldn't wrangle her. It's easier to get a feral cat into a carrier than it was to get my nana to move into an assisted-living facility or stop keeping her cash hidden in tinfoil in the bottom drawer of her stove.

After she suffered a rather touch-and-go bout with pneumonia in her midnineties, I really thought Nana would finally acquiesce to a nice assisted-living facility. But she balked at the idea of even going to physical therapy to get her knees working again. "Rehab?" she said. "No. I'm not going to rehab and sit around with a bunch of druggies."

Nana eventually allowed a visiting nurse to come check in on her once a day but it ended up exhausting her more than helping, because she spent so much time cleaning her house in preparation for the visit—or, as she referred to it, "this rude woman who barges into my house and wakes me up when I'm sleeping and asks me about my poop."

Maybe it's a generational thing. Nana, after living as a widow for over thirty years, took great pride in running her own household. No man was there to tell her what to cook for dinner—or even to cook dinner. She'd given her life to her husband and her children and she wasn't about to relinquish authority over her own remote control to some caretakers in an assisted-living facility. She was free to have a dinner of black tea and saltines while listening to her favorite radio show about aliens and conspiracy theories. Unlike my nana, I would live in an assisted-living facility now if my health insurance would cover it.

I used to tap-dance in nursing homes when I was in middle school—because I was both a humanitarian and a giant loser. Sure, people were drooling and struggling to hold their own heads up, but they seemed so happy in their oblivion, their only responsibility to clap and make the buck-toothed girl with the too far apart eyes feel good about herself. Or maybe they actually enjoyed my tap interpretation of Elvis Presley's "Blue Suede Shoes." I think it must have been the drugs.

I have a nice apartment. It's spacious and I love my furniture and my framed magazine covers from the 1960s that adorn my walls, but if someone offered me the opportunity to live in a luxury hotel with an on-call nurse to sponge-bathe me and open my mail, I'd say, "See ya later, dust den." The thought of living somewhere where I'm brought pills that make me sleepy and I'm seated in front of live entertainment every afternoon at four o'clock makes me all misty because, unless I fake a nervous breakdown, I'm very far from the age where such accommodations are appropriate. I definitely want to be taken care of when I'm old—by a team of people who hand out heating pads and pudding *for a living.* If I have a kid just for the sake of having a late-life nursemaid and he grows up to be a web designer, what good is he? He doesn't have a prescription pad or a stable of teenage-but-legal boys who are willing to "dance" for an old lady.

It's hard for me to commit to something today just because it might serve me in the future. It's like exercising now so that my knees feel good when I'm old. Who cares? I'll want to just sit down when I'm seventy-five anyway. It's hard for me to even picture my future—besides the future I always picture, which is that I am retired by forty and living in a "community" in Palm Springs. It's also somehow magically 1970-something and I'm hosting pool parties at my ranch-style house for the likes of Liza Minnelli and whoever her gay husband is at the time.

I've always been somewhat of a believer that the world will end in my lifetime. Maybe it was from watching that fucked-up *Day After* movie or maybe it's because the polar ice caps are melting and the world is *actually* ending. There was a tornado in Brooklyn in 2010! I don't go so far as to jar my own urine and keep it in my basement (I don't have a basement), because unlike these professional "doomsday preppers," I don't like to plan. I don't even plan for a future that I plan on living in—let alone plan for a future that takes place after the apocalypse. After a nuclear bomb drops and our glowing brains are on the outside of our foreheads, or the aliens land and make us their bitches, do I really want enough bottled water to keep me alive? What's there to live for? Eventually the ice cream is going to run out.

I cashed out three 401(k)s in my twenties because I needed the money right away. I had the same phone conversation with every Fidelity representative.

"Hi. I'd like to cash out my 401(k). I'd love to not have to work as a temp in New York City for about a month. The other day at one of my assignments, the office manager placed a coffee and bagel order for everyone and excluded me. I don't even have my own desk. I have to sit in a chair at a file cabinet. I have nowhere to put my legs."

"Ms. Kirkman, if you are under the age of fifty-nine, you will lose thirty to forty-five percent of that withdrawal in taxes and penalties."

"I am twenty-five years old and have no concept of living until age fifty-nine. At that point I figure I won't have to worry about money because I'll be dead or married to a rich guy, preferably a rich dead guy."

"Okay, Ms. Kirkman, I need to advise you that cashing out your 401(k) can be more expensive than using credit cards to get by."

"My credit cards are maxed out so I won't be using them to get by. How soon can you send me the money? There are a ton of designer knockoff purses for sale on Canal Street but I don't think the guy is going to be at his table for long. The police have really been cracking down on fake Kate Spades."

"Ms. Kirkman, if you cash out your 401(k), you are restarting the clock on your retirement date."

"I hate the thought of my money sitting there while I'm young and having fun. It's not cool. These are the best years of my money's life—I want it to be free with me. It's not fair to keep those bills all cooped up only to let them out when I'm elderly. I won't be able to keep up with it. That's not fair to my money. Money needs a young mother who can walk up and down Canal Street with it, looking for purses without using a cane."

WHEN I GRADUATED from college, I began planning for my future by securing the following credit cards: Victoria's Secret (everyone needs underwear!); Bath and Body Works (everyone needs chemically induced pumpkin-scented shower gel!); Limited Express (everyone needs tight polyester shirts that don't breathe!); Macy's (everyone needs somewhere to go to buy their mom a Christmas gift!); and Sears (because it sounds grown-up; it's where adults go to buy their barbecue grills and those picks that hold corn on the cob that nobody uses). At age thirty-four, when I finally finished paying off the last of my debt incurred by interest on never-paid-off charges for lacy thong underwear and stretch pants, I vowed to never use credit cards again. I now have one that I use only for travel and emergencies. And my emergencies never involve needing a last-minute lawn chair or raspberry foot spray.

I finally have a great work ethic. I write full-time on a TV show. In my spare time I write and perform stand-up all over the country. I'm writing this book in between moments of procrastination when I'm reorganizing my closet and cleaning each individual key on my computer keyboard with its very own Q-tip that's been dipped in Windex. Back when I had my first job as a box office representative at the Boston Ballet, I got bored after a week of doing the same thing every day—and that same thing was . . . working. I called in sick, claiming that I had mono. Mono lasts six to eight weeks and is highly contagious. Mono makes the sufferer so tired that she can't get out of bed. Coincidentally, that is also a symptom of lethargy and depression.

I lay in bed for two days with "mono" until I walked into my kitchen to light a cigarette from the pilot light on the stove and a mouse ran over my foot. I steadied myself by putting my hand on the counter. Crunch. I broke the back of a cockroach with my bare hand. The cockroach ran under the microwave (with a fucking broken back!). Both critters got away because they are faster and have stronger constitutions than human beings. Here they were showing up for work every day and I was avoiding my job, pretending to have mono because I wanted to sleep for fifteen hours a day. Terrified of my own apartment, I got the fuck out of there, returning to work that afternoon, having made a miraculous "recovery."

(By the way, this is another reason that I don't understand people who want to stockpile bottled water so they can survive the apocalypse. Cockroaches are said to be the only things that would make it through a nuclear holocaust unscathed. So if you're one of the lone humans who make it, you'll be sharing a microwave with a cockroach—just like I did when I lived in a crappy apartment in South Boston in 1998. And no matter how many kids you have to ensure that you're taken care of in the future, your stockpile of canned soup and babies can't stop doomsday. You might want to adopt some cockroaches instead.)

EVEN WHEN I was married I was well aware of the fact that having a husband was no guarantee that I'd have someone to take care of me when I grew old, because men die first. Seriously. I'm not a sociologist but look at the math. I grew up with two grandmothers and no grandfathers. I know my personal experience doesn't make my hypothesis universally true, but my favorite kinds of "facts" are the ones that I get to decide are "true." Most people my age have grandfathers who died around age sixtysomething and their wives went on to live another twenty or thirty years. I picture God dictating a memo one day to his archangels:

Dear American Housewives from the 1940s:

I royally fucked up! You had absolutely no rights and no choices in life. It was a total man's world! Oy vey, you gals must hate your husbands, who pinch their secretaries' asses at work all day and then come home and expect you to have dinner on the table. At night they lie on top of you, grunting for a few minutes until they're done, never letting you experience a real orgasm. Okay. Here's what I'll do. I'll come get your husband this year. I'll send an aneurysm his way at age sixty-two. It'll be quick and painless. And then, here, honey, here's the channel changer. You can sit right here in this recliner for the next thirty years or so in peace. You don't have to cook for anybody anymore and I promise I will never let The Price Is Right *be canceled—I'll just keep having different people host every decade or so. Again, I'm so fucking sorry. Huge oversight. My bad.*

GOD

(I know that sometimes women die first, but it has very little impact on the man's future. When a man's wife dies, he just gets remarried three days later because he doesn't know how to use a dishwasher.)

Knowing my theory, some of my friends asked me how I felt about the fact that without kids, I'd likely die a lonely widow. Um, I don't have to live alone just because I'm widowed. I knew when I was walking down the aisle that after my husband died of an aneurysm at age sixty-two I'd just move in with a woman. I don't mean that in a lesbian way. I will just move in with a lady and we'll water plants together. I mean, if she wants to go down on me, that's fine, but I'm not going to do anything to her. I have no interest in going exploring inside another woman's vagina. I have one and I'm freaked out by the weird things that can come out of one—unexplained moisture, once-a-month bloodbath, and the weirdest of all, another human being.

Unlike Best Buy Bren, I grew up on a solid diet of *The Golden Girls*. It wasn't just a sitcom to me—it was a blueprint for my future. I pictured living in my old age with my childhood best friends, Tracy and Shannon. I wasn't sure which of our moms would fill the Estelle Getty role but I always secretly fantasized it would be Tracy's mom because she was the most liberal. She put Tracy on birth control when she was a teenager and accepted the fact that teenagers were sexually active. I felt Mrs. Bowen would be the least likely to judge elderly Shannon, Tracy, and me if we took home any Viagra-popping octogenarian men to our wicker-furnished, pastel-wall-papered home. Tracy and Shannon are both now happily married with children but we can probably still shack up *Golden Girls* style in 2042—because no matter what kind of developments happen with stem-cell research, men will always die first. That's a fact.

DURING THE "Stand-there-and-we'll-form-a-line-and-hug-you-because-you-just-got-married-and-we're-exiting-the-chapel" part of my post-wedding ceremony, one of my dearest friends, Morgan, whispered in my ear, "I'm so happy for you and I just realized I'm gonna die alone."

Morgan is hilarious and if she hadn't mentioned something morose and inappropriate in the moments between my wedding and the reception, I'd have felt let down. I'd much rather consider Morgan's lonely death than suffer through a friend of the family hugging me tight and singsonging into my ear, "Be careful on that honeymoon! Those babies will start arriving sooner than you think!" I wanted to whisper back to that woman, "Oh, don't worry. I don't want kids. We'll be relying on my birth control pill *and* pulling out. But just in case, not only have I researched great luaus on the island of Kauai, I know every Planned Parenthood–type establishment within a five-mile radius of our hotel. And if I can't get an appointment, think of how lush and tropical the flowers are that grow between the cracks of the cement in the back alley where I'd get that Hawaiian honeymoon abortion."

But those words "I'm gonna die alone" stuck with me through the reception as I Vogued with my mom on the makeshift dance floor at a colonial inn in rural Massachusetts. Dying bothers me—a lot. But aren't we all going to die alone? Death is like getting a ride to the airport. Sure, someone can escort you to the curb, but it's against the law/laws of nature for your ride to see you all the way through to the departure gate/pearly gates. The scariest part of death for me is not the moment when I might feel pain, gasp for my last breath, and shut my eyes forever (or leave them permanently popped open, staring, like all of the bodies that are found in the woods on *Law & Order*).

The scariest part of death for me is the afterlife. Part of me hopes that there is an afterlife because I mostly enjoy being conscious, and if the afterlife is one big feel-good session where there is light 24/7—just like what happens in Alaska for a few months out of the year—count me in. But part of me is nervous that if absolutely nothing happens when we die—if it's just lights out and you're not even aware you're gone—I would still somehow be *aware* that there is no afterlife. I'd be in the dark thinking, *Well. Here I am. In the nonafterlife. In the pitch darkness. Doing nothing. All by myself. What time is it? How long is this going to go on?*

This might be because when my mom would tuck me in at night I'd ask her, "What happens after we die?" and she'd tell me that we go to heaven to be with God. She said it was just pure happiness. There was no stress in heaven and angels sang and we felt peaceful all the time. I asked her how long we stay in heaven. And she got very close to my face, rubbed my head, and said, "Oh, you never, ever leave heaven. You are there for all of eternity and eternity never ends. It goes on and on and on and on and on and on and on and on . . ."

On and on and on? Wait a minute! What if I started to get bored during all of this holy bliss? I could *never* leave? I'd really be happy all of the time? What if I wasn't and everyone in heaven started to annoy me? I'd be in eternity with a bunch of annoying optimists and it *would. Never. End?!?!* Hold on, are there any pamphlets I can read about hell? I'd like to hear all of my options before I commit to any one afterlife real estate.

As you can see, there is not much, including a husband or a baby, that can soothe my irrational fear that the afterlife is a never-ending office party where people seem happy and I stand back watching, wondering, *Is everyone really this well adjusted? What's wrong with me?*

And with regard to dying alone, I'm not even sure if I *want* to die with a ton of people around me. What would I want with a bunch of happy, healthy, younger people surrounding my deathbed, all looking on anxiously, waiting for my death rattle? I think dying surrounded by my children would be annoying. It would remind me too much of being a kid and having to go to bed on Saturday nights knowing that my parents and sisters were going to stay up until one to watch *Saturday Night Live.* There were no VCRs, DVRs, or Hulu yet, so I wouldn't have been able to catch up with it the next morning. Dying with my children surrounding me, I'd think, *This is what motherhood is all about. I birthed these kids. I raised these kids. I sat home at night worried about them while they were out having fun and breaking curfew. Now that I'm old enough to party with my kids, God is being the biggest buzzkill parent of all, calling me home for my curfew, and I'm missing out on all of the fun. My kids are sitting here so that I am not alone when I die but really they're just rubbing it in my face that they get to stay and I have to leave.*

I've told my friends who fear dying alone that if they never have a child who will take care of them in their old age, they can come to my place, provided that they bring their own cot on which to take their last breath and some kind of attendant who can take care of the body. I will sit with them until almost the very end and at the moment when their soul is about to pass I will quickly pull out a cardboard cutout of myself, place it in front of their fading eyes, and run out my back door to avoid hearing the death rattle of a good friend.

I didn't like the movie *Stand by Me*. I was terrified that any second those boys would stop bonding and find that body. I do not like dead bodies. I know that you're thinking, *Nobody likes dead bodies, Jen*. I beg to differ. Some people perform autopsies for a living! Nobody is making them do it! Some people even put makeup and wigs on dead people for a living—I'd be too scared to be alone in a mall, working as a mannequin dresser. Recently, in the Hollywood Hills, some hikers found a human head in the woods on the side of the trail, after their dog sniffed around and pulled it straight out of the plastic bag in which it was hidden. This is why I don't have a child, or a dog. Both of them always want to play with things that aren't toys—like Mommy's vibrator and plastic bags filled with heads.

When I go hiking, I want to look straight ahead and listen to a Dr. Wayne Dyer self-help podcast. I want to get contemplative or listen to Madonna and pretend that I'm in a music video. I have no time to stop and let my pet/kid off its leash so it can run to the edge of the woods and start playing with body parts. I'm not going to wear a fanny pack just so that I can carry hand sanitizer on the off chance that I have to wipe crime-scene DNA off my toddler's tiny hands.

If you're married or have kids, that doesn't mean you won't die alone. You could be groggy from last night's Ambien and mistake a white paper napkin on your counter for a slice of cheese pizza. A few bites in and you start to choke. You collapse to the floor, gasping for breath; the sink is so far away and all you need is some water to wash it down. You eventually give in to the comfort of the white light that you see in front of your eyes. You lay your head down and die, holding on to shards of a half-eaten napkin . . . all of this can happen when your husband is driving the kids to school.

No matter how many assurances you think you might have that you'll be surrounded by and cared for by your children at your last breath, that kitchen floor awaits, ready to take you before your time. I'm safeguarding my home and saving my life by not bringing children into it who will be so messy that I'm required to keep lots of napkins on our countertops. And I take other precautions around the house: I don't engage in any antics like shower dancing or autoerotic asphyxiation. Ultimately, I *am* afraid of pulling a Mrs. Sanders. That's another reason I don't have a dog. If I do fall to my death while changing a lightbulb, I don't want my face to be licked off before somebody comes to find me.

11. It's None of Your Business, but Since You Asked . . .

Feel free to skip this chapter if you've ever been at a cocktail party and asked someone whether he or she wanted to have children, and after that person said no, you pressed on and either told the person what to do (have a change of heart and have a child) or asked follow-up questions such as: "Well, are you open to adoption?" and "What does your husband/mother/father/sister/brother/psychic/proctologist/ mailman say about your selfish refusal to pass on your DNA and contribute to the excessive number of double-wide strollers on narrow city sidewalks, not to mention the selfish preservation of the sanctity of your bedroom by not adding a crib and doing whatever you want with your free time?"

I've worked myself up into a bit of a frenzy and am admittedly heated. So, warning: This chapter might not be for you if you've ever asked someone whether he or she wants to have children and after that person says no, you've tried to guess *why*, didn't listen to the answer, and instead offered unsolicited advice on how to still make it work, such as:

"Don't worry about the money now. Just get pregnant and it will all work itself out."

> *"You should freeze your eggs because if you're feeling like an empty soulless husk as you get older, it will be too late."*
> *"Not everyone shits in the hospital bed when they deliver a baby. If you poop before you go to the hospital, you'll be fine."*

Most people who don't want kids also don't want to be cornered by strangers at parties who launch an informal investigation into our psyches and backgrounds and decision-making capabilities. It's been proven that vice presidential hopeful Sarah Palin wasn't vetted as extensively as I have been in the company of women who are searching for a yet-to-be-discovered "good reason" why I don't want to have children.

Because a woman might have reached a certain age (at which her eggs are rotting in her abdominal refrigerator) or wears a wedding ring (signifying her clear willingness to settle down with one sexual partner for life and gain some permanent weight around her midriff), people seem to think that it's high time to encourage her to take the next natural step in life: getting nauseated at random scents that nobody else can smell, not being able to have more than one glass of prosecco on New Year's Eve, and experiencing the near impossibility of a sex life for six weeks after the baby is born. Invalidating a woman's life choices by saying things like, "Oh, but you'll regret it if you don't have kids," or, "I didn't think I wanted kids either until I had one," is like me going to an Alcoholics Anonymous meeting and telling the newly sober that eventually when they grow old, they'll want to take the edge off with a little gin and tonic and that if they could only just be mature enough to control themselves, they could go on a fun wine-tasting tour in the Napa Valley.

Ladies, if you have recognized yourself in this chapter, I have news for you: you are not the first person to say these things to us childfree-by-choice-ers and sadly you probably won't be the last. These comments aren't things that I can laugh off, like when your charming toddler tells me that I look fat. (Okay, nobody's toddler said that, but it does sound like something a toddler *could* say.) You are forcing your values onto my life and I know that you don't think you are doing that. I know you think you are saving me from a life of childfree loneliness by telling me what it's like on the other side, but what you're really doing is making me scared of you mom types. I will walk down a dark alley at night and not flinch at the sight of a shady man in a doorway—but if I see one of you coming toward me on the sidewalk in broad daylight while pushing a stroller, I will cross the street.

I BARELY KNOW Eileen. She's a friend of my friend Derek and we were talking at his son's daytime birthday party at Dr. Tea's Tea Garden (a trendy tea shop in Los Angeles where you can order a frozen CapaTEAno). Wait, I'm sorry. I don't want Oprah to yell at me about how I've exaggerated my memoir. Full disclosure: *I* was not talking *with* this woman. *She* was talking *at* me. Seemingly unprovoked, Eileen delivered a passionate monologue about how she thought that she never wanted kids until she and her husband accidentally got pregnant and now she can't imagine her life without baby Henry.

"Once we *got* pregnant, we thought, *This is a miracle! Having a baby is absolutely what we were supposed to do!*"

Oh, Eileen, you say "miracle" . . . I say one drunken night your birth control pill rolled under the sink and you said, "Just come inside me. I don't feel like wiping anything off my stomach afterward."

It's not a "miracle" that when you have unprotected sex in your thirties a baby gets made even though you always thought you didn't want one. Babies are not analogous to your drunken cousin whom you didn't expect to appear on your doorstep on Christmas Eve. (Except that they might be equally as needy.) And baby Henry did not show up like the Virgin Mary on a piece of toast. It's science.

Also, would all couples kindly stop saying "we're" pregnant? "We're going to have a family" is fine. But only one person is actually pregnant, which is the medical term for "knocked up." If her

husband gets lung cancer in thirty years, is Eileen going to appropriate his physical condition as well? She'll grab the elbow of her dear
friends at holiday parties and whisper, "It's stage three. We're dying."
She accidentally got pregnant. Not her husband. If their failed birth
control actually produced a growing fetus in her husband's nonexistent womb, then they need to pitch a reality show ASAP. Episode
one can probe this phenomenon and show how hard it is to raise
two babies when both Mommy and Daddy have to recover from a
C-section!

Eileen bounced baby Henry in his BabyBjörn. He spit up a little
bit on her hand but she smiled and said to me, "It's all worth it.
Every minute." Then asked, "So, when are you going to have kids?"

I wanted to answer, "It's none of your business, but since you
asked . . . ," and tell Eileen that I didn't really want to find myself
strapped to a poop machine at an overpriced tea shop anytime in
the near future, but in the interest of polite conversation I just said,
"Actually, I don't want kids."

This is where that polite conversation should stop. It should be no
different than her asking, "So, when are you buying a multimillion-
dollar mansion?"

Me: "Actually, I don't want to buy a multimillion-dollar mansion."
Eileen: "Oh, no mansion? That's cool. That's your personal
choice. So, how crazy was *Mad Men* last week? Boy, that
Don Draper sure does like all kinds of midcentury modern
pussy!"

BABY HENRY FIDGETED in his external cotton-womb, trying to
unbutton his mom's shirt. Eventually, like all men, Henry gave up
trying to figure out how to work a hook and-eye clasp and just pulled
Eileen's shirt to the side, located her boob, and put his mouth right
on her nipple. I felt like I was thirteen years old again and watching

Alex the Burnout go up the shirt of Nicole the Skank on the dance floor during Led Zeppelin's "Stairway to Heaven." And just like Nicole the Skank, Eileen the Mom let her date suck on her left one in front of all of her friends.

Eileen seemed sad. The breast that baby Henry's mouth wasn't attached to was kind of . . . leaking. It looked like her nipple had left a sweat stain on her nice afternoon tea party shirt. As she bounced, she let out a few farts that tooted along in perfect time with her rhythm. She didn't acknowledge the farts so I didn't either. Maybe that's why Eileen wanted me to have a baby, even though she didn't know me. Maybe once you're at the point of having a boob that drips like a leaky faucet at parties, your instinct is to proselytize. You'd be more comfortable surrounded by women who are leaking and farting as well. You can harmonize like the Mormon Tabernacle Choir. And then when you're done harmonizing you can go door to door, extolling the virtues of multiple wives for one man who will give him at least a dozen children!

I know that nothing you love comes easy. There's crying, flatulence, and wetness with anything that's ultimately worthwhile. That's how Eileen feels about raising baby Henry and how I feel about spending all of my time working on my career. I wish I could spend less time on it, but I don't make the rules about how much dedication it takes just to get a morsel of success in show business and stand-up comedy. Just like Eileen doesn't make the rules about how much dedication it takes to keep baby Henry alive and happy. Eileen chose motherhood. I didn't. And to me, that's where the conversation ends. That and when someone starts making toot noises out of her butt while I'm trying to eat a cupcake.

Even though I'm the one making this argument, I resent having to refer to my career as my baby in order to explain myself to parents. It suggests that as long as a woman has *something* she feels maternal toward, then she passes as a regular human being. She wants to swaddle her career, so we'll make an exception and give her a pass!

Women don't have to have maternal urges to be women. My

career is not my surrogate baby just like my car is not my surrogate sex slave just because I turn it on and ride it. Men don't call their careers their sons or daughters. A fireman without kids doesn't have to pretend that his job is his baby replacement. *Oh, yeah, when I walk up those forty flights of stairs fighting back the burning and falling asbestos, I just cradle the hose in my arms and think,* This is my baby.

It's a weird thing society puts on us women. They tell us that we can have careers (well, after they told us we could vote—they sort of said it would be okay if we wanted to have a career, as long as we agree to get paid less than a man for the same job), and then they tell us that we aren't real women if we have careers but no babies, and if we dare pick a career *over* a baby . . . we better at least talk about that career like it's a baby in order to blend in and not call attention to the fact that we're selfish women who are not carrying on the human race.

I don't actually feel maternal about my career, although there are similarities to motherhood. Sometimes my career has me out of bed at five in the morning and it doesn't give a shit how much sleep I've had the night before. I have to constantly come up with new things to "play with" or my career gets bored. You'll never see me breast-feeding my desk or taking its temperature rectally, although I am steadfast about wiping it down every day with antibacterial wipes. (Don't worry. I use the environmentally friendly, chemical-free wipes. I want to make a nice planet for other desks to grow up in.) But unlike with motherhood, I don't feed my career. My *career* feeds *me,* and I can't ignore my career because if I do, someone younger and funnier will give it the attention it needs and then she'll get her own sitcom.

I WENT ON a business trip one weekend and the guy who drove the shuttle from the carport to the airport said, "Where you headed?"

"New York City," I told him.

He got all bright-eyed. "New York City. I've always wanted to go there. But I only know about it from *Sex and the City* repeats."

I was delighted. I realized that my subtle streaks of racism had prevented me from ever assuming I'd get to talk about one of my favorite TV shows with a straight, middle-age black guy.

"Can I ask you a question, Ms. New York? Now, let me guess, are you a Carrie, a Samantha, a Charlotte, or a Miranda? Let me see . . ." He took a look at the motorcycle boots I was wearing and said, "Damn, girl, according to those shoes, you ain't any one of those ladies."

I explained to him that it's not comfortable to wear Manolo Blahniks on a red-eye flight and that it's not financially comfortable in general for me to wear shoes that cost a thousand dollars.

"So you'll get to town and see your girlfriends and have some drinks, like a cosmo or even a lemon drop? That's a new one I've heard of," he said.

"Well, I land at five forty-five a.m. at JFK, so I'll probably just try to find a yellow cab and avoid those guys with the duct tape on their 1988 BMWs who call themselves 'independently owned car services.' But then yes, I will probably see my friends that night. I haven't given any thought yet as to what type of drinks we'll have."

I was having fun with my driver, who looked like a world-weary older black guy but had the soul of a 1980s teenage club kid heading to the Limelight. That is, until he said, "Your husband and kids okay with you taking off for this girls' weekend?"

"Well, actually it's not a girls' weekend. I have a business meeting. Anyway, I'm not married and I don't have kids."

"Girl! What you waiting for! You're attractive! You can find a man!"

I'm not sure why this myth exists that only attractive people get married. Have you ever googled "Cracker Barrel weddings"? I told him that I had once had a husband, that that husband and I did not work out, and that I'm very happy because I get to do things like get on a red-eye without asking anyone's permission. Suddenly it seemed like I was slowly falling into the trap of needing the approval of the guy driving the shuttle from my car to the airport.

"But you wanna have a kid, right?" he asked (I was no longer

fooled by the wide-eyed club-kid persona). I told him no. He said, "Hell, what? I have six kids. It's hard to afford them these days and they are a pain in my ass. They have minds of their own, but I love them. They are the light of my life when I go home. What's waiting for you when you go home from New York City?"

"I think some Greek yogurt that hopefully won't expire over the weekend?"

"Girl," he said, "Greek yogurt don't keep you warm at night."

True. In fact, Greek yogurt will not keep me warm at night but it most certainly will keep me *up* at night . . . with stomach cramps, because I'm lactose intolerant, but I refuse to acknowledge this fate. But when I'm tired and coming home from a business trip on a Sunday at midnight only to have to turn around and be at work by nine o'clock the next day—I would avoid both active cultures and tiny active human beings at all costs.

I WATCHED BABY Henry suck away at Eileen's nipple and, just like I did at the eighth-grade dance after no boy asked me to dance during "Stairway to Heaven," I felt uncomfortable and excused myself. "Well, Eileen. I'll let you go. You seem busy."

She ignored my hint and picked right up where she'd left off before the boob hijacking. Henry kept eating his lunch while I kept missing the passed plates of tea cookies.

"Well, Jen, having a baby is definitely something you can only plan so much. Nobody is really ever ready. There is no perfect time to try to have a baby. You just have to jump in and try."

I'm sorry, what? You *have* to plan a baby. It's the most important decision a human can make! I'm just some selfish woman with a lack of maternal instinct and even *I* know that you should at least *try* to plan for a baby. Buying a vintage Fonzie lunch box at a yard sale you just happened to walk by is something you can't plan a perfect time to execute. Those are the only kinds of miracles that just happen.

"Well, okay, but I think the perfect time to try to have a baby should at least start with someone *wanting* a baby, which I don't."

She eyed me with that vaguely condescending mom look. "I know you love your cute figure and trust me you don't get that back after you have a baby, but once you have kids you realize that there's more to life than fitting into skinny pants."

"Tell that to David Bowie," I joked. "I mean, he'll destroy his whole legacy if he starts walking around with side fat over his leather pants. Nobody wants Ziggy Stardust to turn into . . . Ziggy."

Obviously if I *wanted* to have a baby, and I *could* have a baby, I would fucking have a baby! But I am *never* going to throw away my leather pants from 1997.

"Look," I said, "my not wanting a baby has nothing to do with not wanting to gain weight. I just don't want a kid. But even if I did want a kid, I'm really not the best person for the job."

Baby Henry slapped his tiny-but-stronger-than-a-robotic-claw hand over Eileen's mouth and held it there. He squealed with delight and for no apparent reason, one second later, burst into sobs. With Henry's miniature fingers acting like a fleshy muzzle, Eileen mumbled out the best she could, "Jen, somewhere deep down, you want a baby, but you're scared. I think you doth protest too much."

I don't know what's worse: the fact that she talked only about her kid during an entire birthday party and that my saying I don't want kids just opened me up to a half-hour psychoanalysis session—or the fact that it's twenty-first-century America and she just said "doth."

I wanted to join baby Henry in his tantrum. I don't want to have a baby but sometimes I want to *be* a baby because it's socially acceptable for them to cry and scream in public. I wanted to blurt out, "Oh yeah? Well, I think that *you* doth protest too much and you don't diet enough! Somewhere, deep doth down, you want to go to Weight Watchers and fit into those skinny jeans again but you don't have the stamina! You know you think about skinny pants as much as any other woman. You're a female living in Los Angeles and I'm supposed to believe that you're the *only* one without some kind of body image issue?"

Eileen was right about one thing. I was letting myself engage in this type of confrontation and get defensive again. I was "protesting too much." I should have walked away the minute she said, "I think you'll want a kid now that all of your friends are starting to have them, no?" If she were a lawyer, the judge would have slammed the gavel and said, "Please rephrase the question. Don't presume that the witness wants to have a kid. You doth lead the witness."

Next, Eileen did this thing that pregnant women and moms do; she started in with her war stories. (Some alcoholics do it too at parties when they notice you're drinking and they can't.) They pitch it like some kind of cautionary tale but really I think it's just a way to brag that they've been through some hell that you haven't and you *still* won't be a real person until your body is physically altered by birth or you've woken up in an alley in Tijuana with a sore taint and a new pet donkey.

As though she were granting me just one tiny hint of validation, Eileen confessed, "Well, at least you don't have to pee every five minutes. That's one good thing about not having kids. All I do is pee. I think it permanently affected my bladder. I can't believe it but I've even started having to wear one of those little maxi pads in my underwear even when I don't have my period, just in case some urine falls out."

Falls out?!

When I was in first grade we had a bathroom inside of our classroom. The door must have been made of something very soundproof because none of us six-year-olds were self-conscious about going pee-pee or poo-poo in the private bathroom during class, except for this one kid, Scott Nelson. Scott was obsessed with all things "bodily function." He pressed his body up against that bathroom door anytime someone went inside. He cupped his hands to his ears and you could see the strain in his face as he tried to hear a note of a fart or the crescendo of a urine stream.

When Amanda Jones was out sick for a week with the measles, we were assigned to write her get-well cards. Scott's card was a picture of a bum sitting on a toilet. He drew an arrow pointing at the butt hole with a very educational but not quite get-well message, POOP COMES OUT HERE. It seems like when a woman gets pregnant, her inner Scott Nelson takes over and suddenly sentiments like this become polite party conversation.

I guess because the pressure on a pregnant woman's bladder is for the greater good of bringing life into the world, we should all just sit back and hear about how when they puke they pee and when they pee they fart and when they fart they actually shit their pants. Can't pregnant moms just sit around and talk about civilized things like macaroon cookies—are the ones from Paris really the best? Or debate about their favorite Kennedy brother, or lament that because it's not the 1970s it looks stupid to wear a hair scarf? Why do pregnant women want to tell me at parties that lately they are secreting a starchy white fluid about once a month that causes their underwear to crust? Especially when I'm trying to eat a cream cheese finger sandwich? Scott Nelson was a troubled probable future serial killer when he wanted to talk about what comes out of his butt—what's *your* excuse?

Eileen's exposed left nipple seemed to be a beacon of light for other mother ships at the tea lounge. Suddenly, I was surrounded by a handful of women breast-feeding their young and a handful of women still incubating theirs. One pregnant woman leaned over and said to Eileen in this ridiculous stage whisper, "You were right, girl. I'm horny *all the time.*"

Listen, it is scientifically proven that pregnant women get super-horny because it helps them hold on to their mate who impregnated them. If they weren't horny, their mate would just be living with an overweight pickle eater who stopped shaving her legs. Yet every pregnant woman tells anyone who will listen (I'm looking at you, Jessica Simpson) that she's eight months pregnant and has never felt sexier or hornier! Guess what? If you *didn't* feel sexy or horny during your eighth month of pregnancy—you'd be crying in a ball on the bedroom floor, clutching a snot-filled tissue and wearing your food-stained fleece pajama bottoms as your cheating husband walked out the door with your nonpregnant Pilates instructor. It is not interesting that you are horny when pregnant. If I want to watch women talk about sex openly, I'll watch *The Golden Girls* episode where they go on a cruise and decide to buy condoms and Blanche makes that impassioned speech over the loudspeaker.

When did toilet talk become acceptable daytime party chitchat? When I was on ADHD medication I was so constipated that I had to shove a suppository up my ass. I didn't tell the girls at the stupid fucking tea party this fact. In fact, I have never told anyone that. Now I'm just telling you to brag about how I've never told anyone. Is this what Stockholm syndrome feels like?

Another semiacquaintance, Ali, said to me, "Jen, you're getting the perfect training for motherhood at this party!"

Eileen fielded that one. "Oh, hah, Jen doesn't think she wants children."

Ali looked confused. "Why don't you *think* you want children?"

"I . . . actually . . . I *know* that I don't want children," I said.

Ali shifted her bundle of joy to her other boob. "Well, I mean, can you physically not have children?"

Oh, that's a polite party question! Are you barren? Maybe I am barren. I don't know. I've never taken a test. I have taken an AIDS test twelve times because I really care whether I have AIDS. I have never taken a fertility test because I really don't care whether I am fertile. I told Ali that I assume I am perfectly able to carry a child, especially since my childbearing hips kept me from becoming a professional ballerina, but I wasn't planning to test them out.

Ali and the other mothers exchanged a look. "But, so . . . you'll adopt, right?" She seemed pleased to have solved my problem without a pesky series of IVF treatments.

Adoption is a wonderful thing. Especially if you're Madonna or Angelina Jolie and you can take a private jet along with some private paparazzi to a third world country and pick out a beautiful baby while wearing designer aviator shades and couture khaki pants. What I don't understand is that when I tell people that I don't want to have kids—they immediately think I mean I physically *can't* give birth. I don't know how to be more clear about this. I do not want to make a child nor do I want to pick out a child like I'm at a cabbage patch or a Cabbage Patch Kids convention. It's just this simple: I do not want to raise a child.

Ali warned me in a whisper, "But you could . . . regret that decision." She seemed horrified, like if someone whom she is six degrees of friendship separated from ever regrets not having a baby, she'll be personally affected and have to go on Prozac to deal with her feelings.

"Look," I said, "I've been through worse things than regret and I think I'm old enough to have a pretty good hypothesis on this one. I'd rather regret not having a child than having one."

Ali interrupted, "Oh, but you wouldn't regret having one!" That's when her little girl Marta pointed at my face and said, "Why do you have ugly red dots on your cheek?" Ali and the Mommies shared a mutual chuckle. Ali acted as if her child pointing out my acne was just the revelation I needed to change my mind. She said, "See? Kids keep ya honest and grounded."

Honest? Her kid pointed out my PMS breakout. That's rude, not honest. And I don't need a kid to "keep me grounded" when I have adult acne itself to do that. Oh, boy! Just imagine how much worse off I'd be without kids—I'd be walking around feeling good about myself at a party!

I'm not offended by what a toddler says to me. Her brain isn't fully developed yet. And judging from the behavior of her mom, it probably never will be. But some parents become so rude once they have kids. How about a simple teachable moment for little Marta? Could Ali not have said, "Honey, we don't point out things we see on people's faces unless we're helping them." For example, "You have something white and crusty on your chin, I think it's toothpaste. God, I hope it's toothpaste." (Dog owners are the same way, incidentally. They can't stop their animals from behaving badly and they never apologize for their little ones who can't speak. Meanwhile, I'm left with an unwanted wet nose sniffing around my crotch in public.)

At this point I hadn't been to a birthday party for a friend that started at two and ended promptly at five since *I* was a kid. If you're going to have an afternoon birthday party to accommodate you and your friends' new lifestyles as parents—just go all out and have the damn thing at a park or a playground or something. There's nothing fun about trying to drink a hot tea while toddlers crawl underneath me as though my legs are a jungle gym. (And speaking of jungle gyms, when I was a kid all I saw when I saw that thing on the playground was a death trap. Let's get the kids all loaded up on sugar and send them outside to hurl their bodies around some lead pipes! We'll build it over some brain-busting concrete to catch their fall!)

SATURDAYS ARE MY day to write or run errands, and in Los Angeles if I time it just right, I can hit the dry cleaner and the grocery store—both only two miles from my house—and it only takes six hours with traffic. I had to basically lose a day, like some punishing form of daylight savings, just to see my friend on his birthday. The mothers in the crowd were doing what they would be doing on a Saturday anyway, breast-feeding their babies and changing diapers—except they wouldn't be doing it on a quaint café table for two in public. That's the thing that happens when your friends and acquaintances start to have kids. You have to get on their schedule, like you're a nurse working in a hospice, or the friendship dies on a slow morphine drip—without the fun of a morphine drip.

By this point I felt self-conscious staying at this party without my boob hanging out. It reminded me of an after-hours party I went to in 1986, following Eileen Rosenstein's bat mitzvah, when a bunch of girls retreated to Eileen's room to show one another their burgeoning breasts. Mine were yet to grow. I actually got one boob at age twelve and the other one didn't grow until age fifteen. Every year I went to my pediatrician and asked her what the hell was going on. She always told me that to have one boob grow at a time was normal. Every year I took exception. "Normal? Normal? Having one boob is normal? No. Every girl at school has either some or none but nobody has just one! Besides, if it's so 'normal' to have only one boob, why don't they sell slings at Victoria's Secret?"

At times like this, I feel like I don't fit in with society. Both in the mideighties with my one boob and now with two very nice boobs that don't offer sustenance to others, I don't quite feel like a real woman. Even though I drive a nice car and have a job, a manager, a few agents, an accountant, an entertainment and a divorce lawyer, and other "grown-up" things in my life, I still feel like a fraud. I'm always thinking that any day a policeman is going to stop me as I walk down the street and say, "Excuse me, little girl with the big purse? What are you doing? Shouldn't you be in school right now? Where are your parents?"

I didn't even feel like I was acting like a normal kid when I *was* a kid. In sixth grade, the most popular girl in school, Meredith Renner, had a slumber party. Not just a slumber party—it was a costume party/slumber party. And she was rich. She lived in a mini-mansion before they were called McMansions. My mom never let me sleep over at my working-class friends' houses—mainly because the working-class people always had one parent (usually Mom) working some kind of night shift, leaving the other home to supervise. Everyone knows that kids could start a nuclear missile program in the basement while Dad snores away upstairs in front of an episode of *Nightline*, skillfully clutching a can of Bud Light that never spills.

I don't know why Meredith invited me. I had friends but was not one of the "popular girls." I wasn't rich but I wasn't a nerd. I had saved up some babysitting money and purchased a Benetton T-shirt. I think that T-shirt caught her eye and she assumed I was one of them.

Our assignment was to bring a gift for Meredith and to come dressed up as our favorite celebrity for the big event of the party—the costume contest. I came dressed as Groucho Marx. Now, I was not some eccentric kid who watched Marx Brothers movies. (I'm not even an eccentric adult who watches Marx Brothers movies.) I didn't know the difference between Groucho, Karl, and Richard Marx. I thought Groucho was the stork from the Vlasic Pickles commercial ("That's the best-tasting pickle I ever hoid.") My mom had explained to me that the stork was based on Groucho Marx, a very famous comedian. I figured if he was very famous, then everyone at Meredith Renner's twelfth birthday party would know him. My mom said, "Your father has an old suit that would be perfect for this." I wore a wig and a pair of those Groucho glasses with the fake nose and mustache attached. Now you know why they sell those in novelty stores. It's a hot item for tween girls on their way to the birthday party of the year.

The Popular Girls were not wearing costumes when I arrived in full Marx mode. I only brought pajamas. I had no in-between clothes. I didn't win the costume contest. The prize went to Kayley, who revealed that up the sleeve of her Esprit top she had on ten rubber bracelets. This was her Madonna costume. Meredith got a stomachache right before it was time to blow out the candles on her birthday cake and she said that everybody had to go home. Then she said, "Jen, you call your mom first." I was dumb enough to believe that the slumber party really ended until I found out on Monday that after "some girl who came dressed as a guy" left—the real fun began. The Popular Boys were invited over for cake and everybody watched the movie *Girls Just Want to Have Fun*.

I learned something that day. If you put any effort into anything you do and have a strong sense of self to the point where you don't even question your choices before you walk out of the house—you're a fucking weirdo. You'll have a better time at parties if you look and act just like all the other kids—or else you're going to have to call your mother for a ride, or twenty years later if you're still in the wrong costume, you call your friend Sharon to go out for dollar tacos.

Since kids seem to be the only legitimate excuse that adults get to give for leaving parties, weddings, and work early, I had to make up something plausible to get myself out of Exposed-Breast World. I said that I just realized I'd locked myself out of my apartment and my friend had the keys, but she had to give them to me in the next five minutes or else a secret bomb would explode the world.

I felt slightly self-righteous about the fact that the parking lot was full of SUVs with car seats in the back. Not *one* Toyota Prius or van fueled by cornstarch and weed. Every mother at that party was *sooooo* concerned with her child's future (We have to breast-feed or else their immune systems will be compromised!), and so concerned with my unborn children's future (You aren't having kids? But if people don't have kids, how will the human race survive?), yet none of them cared enough to drive a car that didn't pollute the air that their precious little Martas would breathe once they were old enough to know better about calling me out on my adult acne.

I personally don't believe that the world needs any more people. We are overpopulated as it is and since the advent of the Doritos Locos Tacos Supreme, many folks in our population are the size of two people. But I'm not trying to act like some environmentalist hero just because I don't have a kid. It is not why I'm making the decision, it just happens to be a nice perk of my decision. I did read, however, that even if you do drive a Prius, you are in no way balancing out the carbon footprint that having a kid leaves on this planet. I either read that or I just believe that. Who cares? I'm probably right. Anyway, apart from being the person who turns the switch in the toxic plastics factory with the deregulated smokestack to "on"— having a kid is the worst thing you can do to the environment. Still, I'd never tell someone that at a party because I am a polite adult, not a self-righteous thirteen-year-old (anymore). I was that cashier at Roche Bros. grocery store who rolled her eyes when forced to ask, "Paper or plastic?" I used to stomp my Doc-Martened foot and yell at my boss, "But if we don't give them an option and just give them paper, we could save this world!" I was also that cashier who let out an audible sigh and uttered, "Oh, that's *real responsible*," under her breath after the customer chose plastic.

I like to leave that inner thirteen-year-old girl at home when I go to sophisticated tea parties. She's even more of a buzzkill than a circle of mommies who, instead of asking, "Would you prefer paper or plastic," ask, "Would you prefer a baby or a lifetime of never knowing real love?"

Sharon met me at a new Mexican restaurant in town where the seats hang from the ceiling—like hammocks for one. The waiter kept telling us it was "really chill" but it wasn't that chill, because if you talk with your hands, you start spinning around and it feels like you're a potted plant in a macramé ceiling holder. (If you grew up in the 1970s, you'll know what I mean.)

The waiter tried to flirt with us but we let him know that we were more in the mood for bitching and maybe some crying on the side.

"They make me feel so bad about my decision," I sniffled, and worked up to a nice bawling sob. "Not because I have any regrets about not having kids, but I feel like my life [sob] would be easier [snuffle, heave] if I could just [gulping breaths] fit in with everybody else."

Sharon was already pissed on my behalf. She's this tiny little four-foot-eleven comedian who doesn't want kids either and she was pissed on her behalf too. "You don't have to fit in with them in order for them to be able to talk to you. You should have said, 'Fine, why don't *you* have another kid for me if you want another kid on this earth so bad?'"

"I'm just so sick of feeling like such an outsider!" I twirled angrily in my chair-hammock.

Sharon tried to talk me down by getting all "angry *Wendy Williams Show* audience member." "This bitch Eileen is miserable and she knows it. Misery loves company. She wants you pregnant because when she sees that you're not—she forgets that she had options and it makes her question her decision. You're gonna have some hot guy sucking on your tits later instead of some baby, okay?" Sharon tried to give me a snap, but her hand got caught in the web of her seat.

"Sharon, no hot guy is sucking on my anything tonight. I just want to go to bed."

Suddenly I had an inspiration. "It's like the word 'queer,' you know?"

Sharon agreed wholeheartedly. "Yeahhh. Totally. It's just like that. Wait. How? I don't get it."

"Well, I used to use the word 'queer' because I'm from Boston and we used to say that word, meaning 'stupid' or like 'someone who likes being in the church choir instead of smoking cigarettes in back of the rectory.' But my gay friends said that word offended them and so I stopped. They said to me, 'Why is it so important to you to be able to use that word?' And guess what?"

"What?"

"I realized that it's *not* important for me to use that word. And I want to say to these women with kids, 'Why is it so important for you that I have a kid? Why is it so important for you to spend your time at a party questioning my life choice?' "

My voice started to break. I was so tired from pretending not to be offended at the party. I was holding back tears. If it's not socially acceptable to not have a baby—it's definitely not socially acceptable to cry like one in your refried beans.

Sharon comforted me. "Jen, it's okay to cry. Wait. Wait. Not yet. Wait until the waiter circles back. You want him to see that you're upset. He might bring us more chips."

I decided it didn't matter that there were no chips left and ate some guacamole with a spoon.

My tears turned to indignant passion. I made a declaration. "Sharon, I think that childfree by choice is the new gay. We're the new disenfranchised group. People think we're irresponsible, immoral sluts and that our lifestyle is up for debate."

Sharon agreed. "That's genius, Jen. Genius!" She started writing on a napkin. It was so wet it ripped. "Ah, fuck it. I'll remember what you said. Something, something . . . the new gay."

We burst into laughter and then let the tears stream down our faces. Sharon said, "I don't want to make you more upset but I have something to tell you."

"What?"

"I saw a BABY ON BOARD decal on a car today. I was trying to pull up beside her but she wasn't noticing. I had my window rolled down. I was all ready to say, 'Hey. This isn't 1985 and nobody gives a fuck.'"

Sharon knew this was something that I loved to hate, including those cars that have the decals that indicate Mommy, Daddy, Timmy, Jill, and the family dog. I also can't stand MY CHILD IS AN HONOR STUDENT bumper stickers.

I'm glad your kid won a spelling bee or gets good grades or that you love being a soccer mom or that you're proud of your kids. Do you really have to put it in bumper-sticker form? Is any kid going to be on a therapist's couch years from now saying, "My parents clothed me, fed me, tucked me in at night, and read me bedtime stories, they paid for my college education, but there is a bumper-sticker-size void in my psyche and a decal-size hole in my heart. I wanted everyone who drove by us on the 10 freeway to know that my mom loved me!"

When I was growing up my parents would have been embarrassed to have bumper stickers on their car that announced their love for their kid. Also they hated bumper stickers. "Jennifah, those are so hard to get off and they immediately decrease the value of the cah. Do *not* go putting one of those Wham! bumpah stickahs on there. When you get your own cah you can deface it any way you like."

Congratulations. You are proud of your Cub Scout. I assume that if you have kids, you're proud of them, so if you keep talking about how proud of them you are . . . maybe *you* doth protest too much? And by the way—while you're busy picking out bumper stickers about Troop 79, make sure your son still wants to be in the Cub Scouts. Maybe he wants to do something else like be a brooding drama club kid or take tap dance lessons after school. Cub Scouts is kind of queer.

UNLIKE THE LOVELY pissed-off Sharon, some friends of mine (and professionals whom I pay to hear me whine) ask me whether I couldn't just humor the moms like you do with Scientologists to get them to leave you alone. Couldn't I just tell them, "Sure, maybe I will have kids/consider the dangers of never getting 'clear' by not accepting Xenu as my lord and savior," and then move on?

What if I were gay and someone said to me, "You'll change your mind"? Would you agree and suggest that I say, "You're right; I will probably stop being gay once I get this immature loving-the-same-sex thing out of my system"?

Sounds stupid, right? Can't people with children accept that we childfree people know ourselves? Why should I have to give in just to make them comfortable? The worst part is I tried that tactic. I've said, "Yeah, maybe," and guess what? They don't stop. The floodgates open and the next thing I know they've set a date for my baby shower. I can never, ever win. Except for the fact that my stomach doesn't look like a deflated balloon. Although it will soon since I keep skipping my Pilates lessons.

It's time for the bullying from breeders to stop. Are children the only thing you guys can talk about? When you're not talking about your own pregnancy you're talking about how everyone else should be pregnant. Did you forget that you used to have interests and hobbies and opinions about things other than my uterus? We childfree ladies are tired of defending our positions on something that doesn't need defending. It's not like we're starting a new chapter of the KKK and telling your kids that instead of dressing up like a regular ghost this Halloween—why not make a cute pointy hat with that white bedsheet?

I'm not trying to be dramatic. Sometimes I really do feel bullied by parents. (Not by all parents. Just the ones who tell me that

I should have children after I tell them that I'm too selfish/skinny/tight-vagina'd to do so.)

I know that we're all grown-ups and no one is pulling my hair (well, some people are but that's not your business) or calling me fat on Facebook or threatening to beat me up. I was bullied in elementary school. I'm not making light of the word "bullied." I fell into a puddle on the playground at recess one day and my clothes were soaking wet so I had to go to the school nurse to get cleaned up. She left me alone in her office to undress. On the cot she'd laid out one of those scratchy gray blankets I'm assuming were donated to American elementary schools from war-torn third world countries.

As I was wrapping this afghan-size Brillo pad around my body, my personal bully, Greg, appeared in the doorway. Short, big-eared, gravelly voiced, Greg saw my naked body just moments before it was covered. He said the worst thing that anyone has ever said to me upon seeing me naked (at least out loud). "Ewwww, gross."

Now, he wasn't wrong. I probably was gross. I had spotty new pubic hair and little nubs instead of boobs. Never having seen a spray-tan booth and it being the dead of winter in Massachusetts, I was most likely a special shade of practically clear pale. But it's still not nice when an eleven-year-old girl stands naked in front of her archnemesis and he says, "Ewwww, gross." And that's how I feel every time a woman I know or don't know says to me, "You'll change your mind," or, "You're selfish." I feel exposed and judged for my totally natural self. And just like Greg—who went on to say, "Ewwww, gross," about three more times, even after I'd put the blanket around me and shrieked, "Get out of here!"—these women continue to stand in front of me and relentlessly repeat their insulting observations. To their credit, at least they don't usually end their bullying monologues with, "Jen, you ah wicked retahded."

It's not like I don't understand where Greg was coming from. He had his own insecurities. Maybe he hated being short or having big ears or a shitty father. I have no idea why he zeroed in on me to pick on. It could have been because I came to school dressed up as Mozart one day for no reason, or the time I wanted to interrupt class to read a poem about a lighthouse that ended up sounding really phallic: "A lighthouse grows between two rocks on a cliff, straight and tall, nice and stiff." That *is* pretty retahded. My very existence confused Greg and pushed some of his buttons. He didn't yet have the communication tools to ask me, *"Why did you cut your own widow's peak on your hairline? Why do you wear bell-bottoms from the 1970s in 1985 and not seem to care that you're out of style? Why doesn't Jen care what I think of her? Does Jen judge me? Oh, I don't want to be judged. I better preemptively strike. Now, where's that snowball?"*

Maybe I need to cut moms a little slack. Maybe the Eileens and Alis of the world stare at me and think, *Why did she get that Joan Jett haircut at age thirty-seven? Why does she wear bell-bottoms and not seem to care that it looks costumey at our age? Why doesn't she want to have a baby? If Jen doesn't want to have a baby—does that mean that she judges me for having one? I'd better preemptively strike. She's not leaving this party until she's as uncomfortable as me—a woman with toddler drool on her tits, a busted bladder, a hot fart coming down the pipe, and a maxi pad in her granny panties.*

Hey, it's none of your business, but since you asked . . .

12. Becoming Miriam

When my sister Violet had stage three breast cancer she didn't be-come a medical marijuana–smoking, mellow, sleepy little patient. The chemotherapy turned her into a superhero—whose superpower was finding household projects that absolutely needed to be done. (They didn't need to be done.) It's hard to wrestle a hammer out of the hands of a determined woman with steroids in her bloodstream and try to tell her that the oil painting of her cat that a friend made does not need to be hung up above her fireplace at this very mo-ment—or ever. (Just so you don't think I'm a total monster—she made a full recovery and she still has her original boobs.) I stood behind Violet while she surveyed the plaster in her wall. I thought of taking a bronze candlestick to her head—just one sharp blow that would either sedate her into a silly grin like a cartoon character or perhaps injure her enough to go to the ER, where she could get some drugs that would ease her pain and get her to calm the fuck down.

I left the house to walk down her long driveway to check the mail. "Jennifah, I told you the mail doesn't come until aftah two o'clock. There's no point in walkin' down there." Oh, there's a point. To get a few minutes' respite from the chemically created Bob Vila–Womanzilla—even if it was a failed mission.

Even though Violet was doing things like telling me to rip the lettuce for her salad more quietly, I felt such compassion for her. The chemo didn't make her nauseated like most patients, it made her irritable. I imagine it was like having a rush-hour Friday traffic jam, a screaming baby on a red-eye, and a fly that won't stop buzzing around your head all pumping through your veins at the same time. What's worse is that she was surrounded by a bunch of friends and family who loved her, but they did not have cancer. She was alone in a sea of smiling faces that couldn't stop asking questions in order to make *themselves* more comfortable. Do you want to lie down? How about soup? Do you think that you need to see a specialist in the city? Have you tried drinking fresh-squeezed orange juice? You should really lie down. Have you thought of joining a support group? Are you nauseous? Will you be nauseous later? Can you spell "nauseous"? There are two *u*s in that word, right?

My sister, who had divorced a year earlier and lived alone, had to suffer through the most annoying question of all during her recovery: "Do you regret not having kids?"

One afternoon Violet and I sat on her couch and watched *Elf* for the second time that day even though it was the middle of July. Our favorite scene is when Will Ferrell is in the waiting room at the pediatrician's and he says to a cute little girl, "I'm a human—raised by elves." And the little girl says in a sweet voice, "I'm a human—raised by humans." We always tear up and say to each other, "Oh, she is *sooo* cute and so sweet. She's just full of wonder and joy because it's almost Christmas. She's so innocent and pure—she doesn't judge Will Ferrell's character, Buddy, for wearing an elf costume because she hasn't even learned how to judge others yet." That's about where our maternal instinct stops. By the next scene we're grossed out by all of the kids who are touching things all over the store and we realize just how many germs we encounter when Christmas shopping.

Violet and I never talk that much about how we both don't want kids. We don't need to, because we both accept and respect each other's decision and we don't need to ask nosy questions we already know the answers to. Plus we're usually too busy quoting lines from

Caddyshack or talking to her tuxedo cat, Miss Mitty. But we definitely bonded over our collective outrage at how people turned her cancer into an opportunity to give her a sideways glance about being child-free at age forty. When my sister told me that some of her friends and even *random people in the waiting room at the hospital* had said some version of, "It's too bad you don't have children to help you through this," I got as angry as a cancer victim who had to suffer the injustice of her little sister making a salad too loudly.

Look, you want to badger a normal, healthy woman about whether she realizes that if she doesn't fix that biological clock, she could run the risk of never having C-section scars or her floppy post-childbirth vagina sewn up in episiotomy surgery like a real woman— that's one thing. But to suggest to a cancer victim that she might suddenly regret not having children, when there is so much else to think about, like oh, I don't know . . . *Am I going to die?* Do I have to stop eating Twinkies? Why *can't* I use this free time off work to hang a paint-by-numbers replica of a cat in the most prominent place in my living room?

What kind of person would seriously wish for a cancer-ridden single woman to add motherhood to her to-do list? Not to mention wish for a child to exist in the world and have to watch her mother lose all of her hair. And oh, what a shame, Violet didn't get to test out her cancer genes on a new generation. Bummer that her daughter won't grow up to maybe also get breast cancer someday! My poor sister—I mean, she had to get in her car and go to chemotherapy without having to strap a child into a car seat. She must have been so *not* put upon by another human who needed her for life sustenance, *and* she had to take naps during the day—because she was too tired to even check her Facebook page to see whether any cute guys from high school were divorced yet—without worrying about a tiny help-less being screaming in the next room. It's morbid but we joked that if she had died, people would be saying, "It's such a shame, there are no kids at this funeral to lighten the mood."

Since Violet was full of vim and vigor and anger-inducing chemo, she actually answered people with things like, "I have cancer. I'd hate for my kids to see me like this and I'd hate to not be able to take care of them because I have to sleep all the time. Besides, I can't even have a lot of visitors because I have a shitty immune system at the moment and kids, being the little germ machines that they are, could possibly kill me right now. So, I'm sorry that you're sorry, but I'm not sorry. Besides, I never wanted kids and having cancer hasn't changed that."

Luckily, my sister Lynne is a mother of three *grown* children and so she had the freedom and time to visit from Vermont to help out and get told by Violet that she wasn't making toast correctly. My guitar-strumming, folk-singing sister Lynne has never questioned her sisters' choices not to have kids. Mainly because she'd rather work in the garden in her backyard, deep in the woods and high in the mountains of Vermont, than bother telling anyone how to live her life. (She knows how complicated it is for us just being aunts. You want to bum a cigarette off your seventeen-year-old niece and ask your nephew in college if he has any pot, but you know it's inappropriate. Just kidding, Lynne!)

Violet confessed that even though she felt sick all of the time from the chemo, she kind of enjoyed the time off from taking care of four horses and working full-time at a brokerage firm. She was tired. (Yes! People without kids also get tired!) And she had enough to deal with—our dad was at her house every day asking the same questions over and over: "Where do you keep your paper towels?" And my mother was saying things like: "Your hospital bills are high, are you sure you want to start buying organic vegetables?"

WHEN I TOLD my parents Matt and I were splitting up, my mom said, "Jennifah, my other two daughters are divorced and now you're getting a divorce? I have to ask you. Was it something your father and I did?"

Most kids worry that their parents' divorce was their fault, but in my world, my parents worried that my divorce was their fault. The divorce was nobody's fault. It was amicable. "Amicable" when used for breakups means: "It's not really your business and this whole thing sucks but I wasn't dumped, so don't pity me."

After convincing my mom that it wasn't anything she did that made me no longer want to be married, she finally concluded, "Well, Jen, this is very Hollywood. It's very hard to stay together in show business. Look at Elizabeth Taylor and Richard Burton. They married, divorced, and then remarried! Their relationship couldn't take the scrutiny of the public eye."

"Mom," I told her, "Matt and I weren't in the public eye. I've never been chased by a paparazzo." She then consoled me, not about the divorce but about my celebrity standing. "Oh, Jen, you will be there shortly. I always run into people who say that they love watching you on *Chelsea Lately*."

I was sitting in my divorce lawyer's office, thinking, *I have a divorce lawyer. This is something that grown-ups have. Well, not every grown-up, but still. I feel like a war veteran. I have been through some shit that not everyone is strong enough to go through. Some people stay married when they're not in love. Some people don't even demand that lots of love exist in their marriage—it's a partnership, a way to raise kids and join incomes. But hey, I'm not a victim. I'm not a hero. I'm just a grizzled old vet who fought for his country/woman getting a divorce.*

Then I caught my grandiose train of thought and abruptly changed gears. *Jen, what are you, five years old, thinking that putting a divorce lawyer on a five-thousand-dollar retainer makes you a grown-up? And speaking of retainers, you wear one at age thirty-seven. Where is it? Your orthodontist told you that you have to wear the Invisalign twenty-two hours a day for one year if you ever want to see that incisor on your top row of teeth move or else it will stick straight out just like your grandmother's. A crooked tooth is fine for her—she lives alone in a nursing home—but you're about to get out there and have meaningless postmarriage sex with young musicians.*

My lawyer took me through the basic questions as he filled out the paperwork for me. Homeowners? No. Age? Thirty-seven. His Age? Thirty-three. Kids? No. Mr. Legal Marriage Ender dropped his pen and looked me in the eye. "No kids?" No. "Did you want kids?" No. "Did he want kids?" No. "Well, if he changes his mind, at least he's young, right?"

I always wondered whether Matt would change his mind about kids if he weren't married to me. I know he said he didn't want kids, and he never had a visible paternal instinct. He cringed even more around babies than he did around cats—and he's allergic to cats. I always predicted that if I died before Matt, in some kind of tragic stand-up comedy accident on the road—like if too much in-flight Klonopin caused me to trip over my carry-on bag as I shimmied out of my seat toward the bathroom and I used the emergency exit door handle to break my fall, causing me to get sucked out of the plane, where I'd free-fall for a bit and have a heart attack in midair, and my lifeless body would flop to its final resting place in someone's backyard in Oklahoma—he would remarry a much younger woman who really wanted a baby. She would have family money and neither she nor Matt would ever have to work again, nor would they have to take care of their own child. Matt agreed with my assessment. The only way he could see himself becoming a father would be after my untimely death and his union with a hot twentysomething and her trust fund.

Mr. Legal Marriage Ender said, "Okay. Off the clock." This was his way of showing me that he was keeping it honest. We were about to talk but it wouldn't be deducted from my retainer (the money one—not the one on my teeth).

"You really don't want kids? Are you sure it wasn't just because you were with the wrong guy?"

"You know," I told him, "I'm actually writing a book about how I never just get to say, 'I don't want kids,' without a million follow-up questions and now this conversation is going in the book."

"What if you get pregnant before the book comes out?"

"Then I hope you'll represent me in the first-ever divorce from a baby."

• • •

NATURALLY, MY FRIENDS were concerned about me after the divorce—not because of the fact that I live in a first-floor apartment in
a complex with no doorman and a very chintzy home alarm system,
making me the perfect victim of a home invasion by either a roving
gang of up-to-no-gooders or an army of superfit, tan L.A. zombies,
but because I was now thirty-seven and childfree, even though I'd
spent all thirty-seven of those years telling them I didn't want children.

I was on a flight after a gig once with my comedian friend Ray,
who couldn't wait for the plane to land so that he could get home
and give his wife and kids a hug. He said to me, "Jen, you were so
sure that Matt was the One—so how can you be sure that you don't
want kids?"

"I wasn't a hundred percent sure Matt was the One," I replied.
"But I took a leap of faith. Romantic love is not parental, instinctual,
unconditional love—it's complex. And what if I change my mind
about having kids and I decide to have one and then I change my
mind *again*? As gut-wrenching (and expensive) as it is to change your
mind about who you love, it's a hell of a lot easier to get divorced
than it is to toss a kid back into the sea and tell them that they'll
meet someone else someday who will really love them."

Then Ray added the kicker, the go-to asinine comment from
parents everywhere who want to induct you into their club of 3:00
a.m. feedings, applying to private pre-preschools, playground concussions, teenage daughter pregnancy scares, and teenage sons who
realize one day that they always wanted to be daughters and hit you
up for money for their transition surgeries: "I'll just feel so sad for
you if you never know the love of a child."

To which I said, "Well, I feel sad for you too. You'll never know
what it's like to fuck a twenty-three-year-old drummer."

• • •

THE FIRST MORNING that I lay in bed without Matt beside me, I decided to go to Starbucks and get a coffee and the *New York Times* Sunday Styles section, and then get back into bed in my clothes and stay there all morning. And yes! I get up at seven on weekends because I love my free time. Not every childfree person sleeps late and parties all the time. I am still a *grown-up*. I was happy. It felt right to be in a big bed by myself. I was relieved that I was on my way to no longer being married. I thought of my old coworker Miriam, who used to read the *Times* every morning in our shared workspace in the basement of the Charles Playhouse in Boston as she balanced a lit Pall Mall cigarette in her mouth.

I revered the way Miriam ashed her cigarette while she counted the one-dollar bills in the cash box. We were box office cashiers, selling tickets to Boston's original long-running dinner theater show *Sheer Madness.* I was twenty-two years old, broke, single, and miserable. Miriam was sixty-two years old, broke, single, and fabulous. Not only did I want to be her when I grew up—I wanted to be her at that moment.

Miriam wore a brooch that on any other woman who doesn't get her period anymore would look musty. She looked fashion-forward. Her nails were painted such a specific shade of retro-red that I'm sure it came from a thirty-year-old bottle of nail polish. She wore a different black dress every day—always a fine wool-cashmere combination, always perfectly tailored. Miriam went to New York City two weekends every month to have dinner with friends and see a Broadway show. She told me that it was easy—just a forty-dollar round-trip bus ride on Greyhound and a very inexpensive stay in a youth hostel. It sounded so glamorous and free-spirited. Years later when I realized you have to share rooms in youth hostels and there are no private bathrooms, I wondered how she possibly could have lived that way. Miriam was the type of woman who, if not obligated by a job sitting behind a card table in a Boston basement every day to make a living wage, would be in a café somewhere just drinking endless cups of black coffee and reading the paper. She had a

European sophistication about her, where she could linger leisurely doing one thing at a time, smoking unfiltered cigarettes and apparently not getting cancer.

I was struck by Miriam's independence. She was divorced and happily never married again. She had no kids. She seemed just as content and natural as other women her age who were grandmothers. I couldn't picture Miriam ever having ugly stained potholder mitts on her red-lacquered hands. Money was saved not for a rainy day but for a few days later at the TKTS booth in Times Square. She was exactly the kind of person a teenager/young adult looks up to. She seemed to be doing all of the things that reminded me of what James Dean did during his years in New York City—taking dance classes, being creative, hanging out with interesting people who knew they were interesting, kissing men.

I smiled in bed as I read Bill Cunningham's column and wondered whether Miriam was still alive. I hadn't thought of her in fifteen years but that day, because of her, I wasn't sad to be alone in bed, reading the *New York Times*. I'd never read the paper with my husband, or any man, as a couple. I cringe at those TV commercials that show couples doing the crossword puzzle together in the morning. I start to get claustrophobic just watching. Can't couples do anything apart? Can't one of them run an errand while the other one chain-smokes at an outdoor café? How do they have all of this free time to waste together? And more important, who has one pencil in their home—*let alone* two?

I always knew that I was a Miriam, but as each year of my life went by I talked myself out of it, thinking that since being a Miriam wasn't what most women did, my reasons for wanting to be like her were probably just immature fantasies or excuses to myself about why I couldn't have a "real" job and a "normal" marriage and family. Parents talk a lot about how much strength and dedication it takes to raise a child. It does. It also takes a lot of strength and dedication to carve out a life that doesn't seem normal to anyone else.

After my marriage ended I found out that I have something in common with moms and dads. Divorcées count time in months just like new parents who say, "Little Jillian is only sixteen months old but she's already reading!" I find myself saying, "It's been nine months since my twenty-month marriage ended and I'm not waking up in the middle of the night with nervous explosive diarrhea anymore!"

People used to ask me whether Matt would regret marrying a woman who didn't want children. I don't know whether my ex-husband has any regrets. I do know that he has to write a letter to Brookstone and tell them to stop sending catalogs addressed to him at what is now just *my* apartment. I also know that, like not wanting to have kids, one of the only other instincts I ever had as a young adult turned out to be correct and it's that I am a Miriam. Miriam is like the silent, fifth character from *The Golden Girls*. She's the spontaneous and unafraid-to-be-alone woman who lives inside all of us. Just like the spirit of God exists even in the most lapsed Catholics— we can access our inner Miriam as much or as little as we want at any given moment in our lives.

I do have one regret, though. I never asked Miriam how she managed not to get yellow, nicotine-stained fingers after smoking her three morning unfiltered Pall Malls.

ACKNOWLEDGMENTS

I'm sure plenty of people will be mad at me for writing about them in a book—even with a fake name. And now everyone else can be mad at me for either forgetting or omitting them from the acknowledgments. I will try to keep this list of people I'm thanking to those who have something directly to do with the book—or else the list is going to go on and on and I'll end up thanking Morrissey or just listing private jokes I have with my friends as if this were a middle school yearbook.

Thank you to Sarah Knight at Simon & Schuster. Because of your lack of maternal instinct, you made me a paid author. Thank you for your smart notes and encouragement to keep this book on target and funny and to take chances. Thank you to my manager, Kara Baker, for encouraging me to write a book about my experience as a childfree chick. Thank you to my agent Simon Green at CAA for your support and for selling this. Thanks to everyone at Avalon and CAA.

Thank you to Chelsea Handler. Let's be honest. Nobody was buying my book ideas before I became part of your show(s). Thanks for everything you've done for me—and for hiring me twice. Before you hired me the first time I was temping in a windowless room. I love you.

Thanks to everyone at *Chelsea Lately*—especially the printer by my desk for printing out the first completed manuscript. Everyone else—thanks for reading things in advance and telling me this isn't a piece of shit that should be thrown away: Chris Franjola, Brad Wollack, Heather McDonald, Fortune Feimster, Sarah Colonna, Jeff Wild, Sue Murphy, Tom Brunelle, April Richardson, Josh Wolf, Dan Maurio, Steve and Andrea Marmalstein.

Thanks to my immediate family for just being you: Ron, Joan, Linda, and Gail; and my nieces and nephews, Buffalo, Ali, and Zac. Thanks to my extended family for just being you. If I list you all by name, this will turn into an encyclopedia. I love you all.

Thanks to my friends who were part of this book, from the child-having to the child-free. I appreciate your reading early drafts and sharing your stories. Margaret Morse, Andrew Donnelly, Sharon Houston, Morgan Murphy, Tami and Tara Fitzkoff, Shauna Beland, Teri McDonald, Paul F. Tompkins, and Janie Haddad-Tompkins. Thank you to everyone who has ever had me on their podcast.

Thanks to "Mr. Bergen." I still have the card.

ABOUT THE AUTHOR

JEN KIRKMAN is a stand-up comedian as well as a writer and regular roundtable guest on *Chelsea Lately*, and one of the stars of the hit spin-off mockumentary show *After Lately*. Jen's latest stand-up album, *Hail to the Freaks* (released May 2011), hit no. 13 on the Billboard comedy album charts. Her debut album was 2006's *Self Help*. Jen is also well known for her role as the narrator in the cult-hit series *Drunk History* from Funny or Die/HBO, which won the jury prize in short filmmaking at the Sundance Film Festival. Every month, Jen makes a storytelling appearance on Paul F. Tompkins's podcast, *The Pod F. Tompkast*, which was hailed by *Rolling Stone* as "the best comedy podcast of the moment." Jen has performed stand-up on *Conan*, *John Oliver's New York Stand-Up Show*, *The Late Late Show with Craig Ferguson*, *Late Friday* on NBC, Comedy Central's *Premium Blend*, and the BBC's *The World Stands Up*. Jen was also a cast member of VH1's sketch show *Acceptable TV*. She did many voices on the Cartoon Network's *Home Movies* as well as Current TV's political cartoon *SuperNews!* *Entertainment Weekly* has twice named Jen as a comedian to watch and the *Huffington Post* has named her one of the top ten comedians to follow on Twitter. Jen tours as a stand-up and is based in Los Angeles.